Spanish Leve

MW01169182

Hola and welcome to Spanish Level 1 !

This book is designed to help beginners, children or adults, develop a solid foundation in Spanish and acquire important basic vocabulary.

This book will teach you **over 400 words** covering a variety of topics such as introducing oneself, family, numbers, colors, food, animals, things around the house and the classroom, nature, activities and much more.

An abundance of fun exercises and easy to follow lessons with pictures give the repetition necessary to help you memorize the new vocabulary.

This book makes learning Spanish enjoyable and accessible for people of all ages and makes a great addition to any beginner Spanish curriculum.

Level 1 focuses on developing a varied basic vocabulary and learning how to build simple phrases. "**Sentence builders**" throughout the book will help you put in practice immediately the newly learned words, with sentences becoming gradually more complex. The workbook ends with a challenging **50 sentences quiz** to go over everything you have learned and includes **an answer sheet** and a **word list** for quick review.

I am thrilled to be part of your language journey and wish you the best with this fun introduction to ***Español*** !

*Keep an eye out for **Level 2** where you will master the most important Spanish verbs, how to conjugate them and even more vocabulary. Check out **Bilingoal** on Amazon for more education and language learning material.*

Mimi,

The polyglot behind *Bilingoal*!

This book

Level 1

VOCAB ⚡ BOOSTER

Coming soon!

Level 2

VERB ⚡ BOOSTER

Level 3

FLUENCY ⚡ BOOSTER

Learn:
- **Over 400 words**
- **Vocabulary in over 20 topics**
- **Greetings**
- **Date, numbers...**
- **Simple conversation**
- **Basic sentence construction**
- **Express likes/ dislikes, what you *would* like...**
- **Practice drills**
- **And more...**

Learn:
- Over 200 of the most used verbs
- Regular, irregular and reflexive verbs
- Conjugate them in the most used tenses
- More advanced sentence structure
- More vocabulary
- Extensive practice drills
- And more...

Learn:
- To speak more naturally and fluently
- Common idiomatic expression
- Common proverbs and sayings
- Common clean slang
- Practical situation practice
- Advanced vocabulary
- And more...

Look for our other books on Amazon:

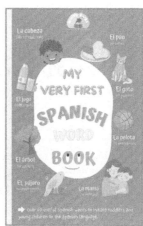

Table of contents

Spanish around the world

Spanish is a romance language (meaning it comes from latin). It is spoken by over 500 million people mostly in South America and Spain and another 75 million as a second language! It is the 4th most spoken language after English, Mandarin Chinese and Hindi and the 3rd most used language on the internet.

Spanish is the official language of over 20 countries and territories, such as Spain, Mexico, Colombia, Argentina and many more! The majority of Spanish speakers live in Hispanic America but Spanish is also spoken by a significant population in other countries such as the United States, Belize, Andorra ...
Spanish is quite a useful language!

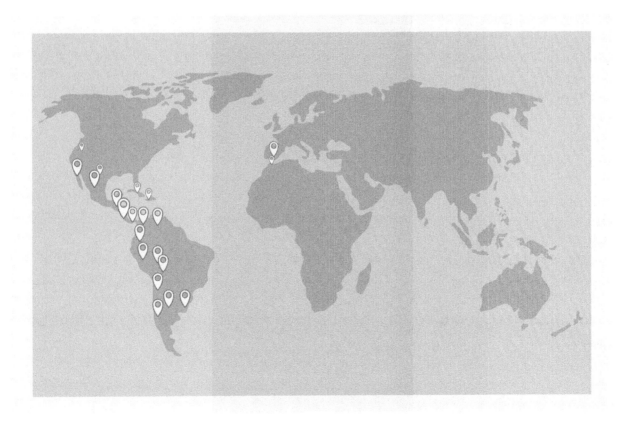

That's over 500 millions Spanish speakers plus YOU! (Very soon!)
So let's get started!

BASICS

Let's get familiar with some important basics:

» **Alphabet and pronunciation:**

El alfabeto (el al•fah•**beh**•toh)

Letter/	Name/	Pronunciation/	Sounds like:
A a	a	(ah)	a in dad
B b	be	(beh)	b in baby but softer in middle of words.
C c	ce	(seh)	s before i and e / k with other letters
D d	de	(deh)	d in dad
E e	e	(eh)	e in fiancée
F f	efe	(EH-feh)	Same as English
G g	ge	(Heh)	Strong H before a /o/ u Otherwise: g in gas
H h	hache	(AH-che)	always <u>silent</u> (except CH)
I i	i	(ee)	ee in see
J j	jota	(HO•ta)	Strong H as Irish "Lo<u>ch</u>"
K k	ka	(kah)	Same as English
L l	ele	(EH•leh)	Same as English
M m	eme	(EH•meh)	Same as English
N n	ene	(EH•neh)	Same as English

Letter/	Name/	Pronunciation/	Sounds like:
Ñ ñ	eñe	(EH•nyeh)	ny in canyon
O o	o	(oh)	o in orange
P p	pe	(peh)	Same as English
Q q	cu	(koo)	k in koala
R r	erre	(EH•reh)	Rolled (as tt in butter in American English)
S s	ese	(EH•seh)	Same as English
T t	te	(teh)	t in taco
U u	u	(oo)	oo in school
V v	ve / uve	(beh) / (OO•beh)	Very soft b
W w	doble ve / uve doble	(do•bleh beh) / (oo•beh do•bleh)	Same as English
X x	equis	(EH•kees)	Same as English
Y y	i griega	(ee GRYEH•gah)	Same as English. It's a vowel & consonant
Z z	zeta	(SEH•tah)	Like the letter S

The following letter combinations are no longer part of the official alphabet but learning their pronunciation is important:

che	che	(ch)	Ch in China
ll	elle	(EH•yeh)	y in yellow (some regions: j in jam)
rr	doble erre	(EH•rreh)	Strongly rolled (trilled)

≫ Diphtongs:

You will often see two vowels combined together within the same syllable. This is called a diphthong. You might know these Spanish words that have diphthongs:

- **Bueno** (bweh·no) *Good*
- **Agua** (ah·gwah) *Water*

Here are some common diphtongs with examples:

Read Y like Y in Yes

ai/ay	aire	(ay·reh)	*air*	**iu**	ciudad	(syoo·dad)	*city*
au	pausa	(pao·sah)	*pause*	**ie**	los pies	(los pyehs)	*feet*
ei/ey	seis	(seh·ees)	*six*	**oy/oi**	hoy	(oy)	*today*
io	medio	(meh·dyoh)	*half*	**au**	auto	(ow·toh)	*car*

- Dipthongs are made of one **weak vowels (i/o/y)** and one **strong vowel (a/o/e)**
- The stress falls on the strong vowel, unless signaled by an accent.
- If two strong vowels are paired, the stress falls on the second vowel. (re**al**) (rreh·ahl)

PS: Every new word is presented with its pronunciation so you do not need to memorize them. You only need to be aware of them.

≫ Stress/Guide:

Word stress means that a syllable in every word is pronounced with a little emphasis, a little stronger. This is very important in Spanish. The rules are:

- Stress is on the **second-to-last syllable** in words ending in a **vowel, N, or S**.
  - <u>a</u>gua (ah·gwah) *Water*
- Stress is on the **last syllable** in words ending in a **consonant (except N or S)**.
  - Com<u>er</u> (koh·mehr) *To eat*
- Stress is on the **syllable** with an accent in words that do not follow these 2 rules.
  - avi<u>ó</u>n (ah·vyon) *Plane*

The part in **bold** in the transliteration (pronunciation guide) indicates the stress.

≫ Nouns:

In Spanish, nouns (people, places, things, ideas..) have a gender: *feminine* or *masculine*.

- **Most** nouns ending in -**o** are masculine: - el niño *The boy*
- **Most** nouns ending in -**a** are feminine: - la niña *The girl*

Articles (the, a...) and adjectives must agree with the nouns in gender and number.

- l**os** niñ**os** pequeñ**os** *The small boys*
- l**as** niñ**as** pequeñ**as** *The small girls*

(Adjectives usually come after the noun.)

≫ Pronouns:

I	**Yo** (yoh)	He	**Él** (el)	You (plural)	**Ustedes** (oohs·teh·des)
You (informal)	**Tú** (too)	She	**Ella** (eh·yah)	They	**Ellos** (eh·yos) (masc) (mixed)
You (formal)	**Usted** (oos·ted)	We	**Nosotros** (no·soh·trohs)	They	**Ellas** (eh·yas) (fem.)

- In Spain, **vosotros** (masc.) or **vosotras** (fem.) is used instead of **ustedes.**
- A few countries in Latin America use **vos** instead of (or in addition to) **tú.**

≫ Verbs:

- Verbs in the "To" form (infinitive) end in -**ar/-er** or -**ir** in Spanish.

  - Habl<u>ar</u> *(To dance)*   • Com<u>er</u> *(To eat)*   • Dorm<u>ir</u> *(To sleep)*

- Subject pronouns (I, You, He...) are often omitted because verb endings (and context) indicate to whom the verb is referring:

  - Habl<u>o</u> (**ah**·bloh) *(I speak)*   The ending "-o" is used for I

- To conjugate (regular) verbs in the **present,** remove the -ar/-er/-ir ending and replace by:

PRESENT		-ar	-er	-ir
I	Yo	-o	-o	-o
You (inf.)	Tú	-as	-es	-es
He/She/ You (for.)	Él/Ella/Usted	-a	-e	-e
We	Nosotros	-amos	-emos	-imos
They/ You (pl.)	Ellos/Ellas/ Ustedes	-an	-en	-en
You (pl.) in Spain	Vosotros/as	-áis	-éis	-ís

You will see these shortcuts throughout the book:

Shortcuts:

(for.) Formal	(mix.) Mixed gender
(inf.) Informal	(m.) Male:
(pl.) Plural	(f.) Female
	(sing.) Singular

Many verbs are irregular in Spanish and do not follow this exact pattern. Our focus in **Level 1** is building **vocabulary**. In **Level 2**, you will study **grammar, conjugation** and learn an abundance of **verbs** to help you speak with more ease.

NOTE: Some Spanish words vary depending on the country. While this book focuses on Spanish from Latin America, you will be understood in any Spanish speaking country.

Empecemos! *(Let's start!)*

Los números (los **noo**•meh•rohs)   – Numbers

» **Read and write the numbers four times:**

1. uno (**oo**•noh)

6. seis (**say**.ees)

2. dos (dos)

7. siete (**syeh**•teh)

3. tres (trehs)

8. ocho (**oh**•choh)

4. cuatro (**kwah**•troh)

9. nueve (**nweh**•beh)

5. cinco (**seen**•koh)

10. diez (d.yes)

A **Write the numbers**

2
3
7
9
1
6
8
10
4
5

B **Connect the numbers**

tres •

siete•

nueve

cinco•

diez •

7
5
1
9
2
6
3
10
4
8

• uno

• cuatro

• ocho

• dos

• seis

A   Read and write the numbers four times:

11. once (ohn·seh)

_____   _____

12. doce (doh·seh)

_____   _____

13. trece (treh·seh)

_____   _____

14. catorce (kah·tor·seh)

_____   _____

15. quince (keen·seh)

_____   _____

16. dieciséis (dyeh·see·seys)

_____   _____

17. diecisiete (dyeh·see·syeh·teh)

_____   _____

18. dieciocho (dyeh·see·oh·choh)

_____   _____

19. diecinueve (dyeh·see·nweh·beh)

_____   _____

20. veinte (beyn·teh)

_____   _____

B   Write the numbers in Spanish:

11 _____   16 _____

12 _____   17 _____

13 _____   18 _____

14 _____   19 _____

15 _____   20 _____

C   Connect the numbers.

dieciséis •   16   • once

                13

diecisiete •   19   • catorce

                20

veinte •   18   • diecinueve

                11

                14

trece •   17   • dieciocho

                15

quince •   12   • doce

Write the numbers three times

0 = cero (seh·roh)

10. diez

20. veinte (beyn·teh)

30. treinta (treyn·tah)

40. cuarenta (kwah·ren·tah)

50. cincuenta (seen·kwen·tah)

60. sesenta (seh·sen·tah)

70. setenta (seh·ten·tah)

80. ochenta (oh·chen·tah)

90. noventa (noh·ven·tah)

100. cien/ciento (syen/syen·toh) (Both are used. Cien is a shorter version)

Count by ten: Say outloud the numbers from 0 to 100.

0 – 10 – 20 – 30 – 40 – 50 – 60 – 70 – 80 – 90 – 100

20. veinte

21. veintiuno
(beyn·**tyoo**·noh)

22. veintidós
(beyn·tee·**dos**)

23. veintitrés
(beyn·tee·**trehs**)

24. veinticuatro
(beyn·tee·**kwah**·troh)

25. veinticinco
(beyn·tee·**seen**·koh)

26. veintiséis
(beyn·tee·**seys**)

27. veintisiete
(beyn·tee·**syeh**·teh)

28. veintiocho
(beyn·tee·**oh**·choh)

29. veintinueve
(beyn·tee·**nweh**·beh)

《 **Copy once.**

✦ Did you notice that even if these numbers are written as one word, they are actually made up of two numbers connected by **i** (ee)
This **i** actually means **y** (ee).
Y in Spanish means "**and**" . So these are actually three words joined together:

• veintitrés = veinte + y + tres *(twenty and three = 23)*

✦ **Y** changes to **i** only between 20 and 30, 120 and 130...

• ciento veint**i**séis = ciento + veinte + **y** + séis

*(one hundred twenty **and** six = 126)*

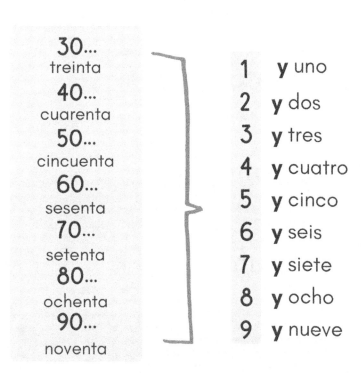

Numbers from 30 to 40, 40 to 50... are written as two numbers separated by Y:

30... treinta	1	**y** uno
40... cuarenta	2	**y** dos
50... cincuenta	3	**y** tres
60... sesenta	4	**y** cuatro
70... setenta	5	**y** cinco
80... ochenta	6	**y** seis
90... noventa	7	**y** siete
	8	**y** ocho
	9	**y** nueve

✦ **Uno** is only used when counting. If you add a noun then use **un** (with a masculine noun) or **una** (with feminine).

30. treinta

31. treinta **y uno**

32. treinta y dos

33. treinta y tres

34. treinta y cuatro

35. treinta y cinco

36. treinta y seis

37. treinta y siete

38. treinta y ocho

39. treinta y nueve

40. cuarenta

41. cuarenta **y uno**

42. cuarenta y dos

43. cuarenta y tres

44. cuarenta y cuatro

45. cuarenta y cinco

46. cuarenta y seis

47. cuarenta y siete

48. cuarenta y ocho

49. cuarenta y nueve

50. cincuenta

51. cincuenta **y uno**

52. cincuenta y dos

53. cincuenta y tres

54. cincuenta y cuatro

55. cincuenta y cinco

56. cincuenta y seis

57. cincuenta y siete

58. cincuenta y ocho

59. cincuenta y nueve

60. sesenta

61. sesenta **y uno**

62. sesenta y dos

63. sesenta y tres

64. sesenta y cuatro

65. sesenta y cinco

66. sesenta y seis

67. sesenta y siete

68. sesenta y ocho

69. sesenta y nueve

70. setenta

71. setenta **y uno**

72. setenta y dos

73. setenta y tres

74. setenta y cuatro

75. setenta y cinco

76. setenta y seis

77. setenta y siete

78. setenta y ocho

79. setenta y nueve

80. ochenta

81. ochenta **y uno**

82. ochenta y dos

83. ochenta y tres

84. ochenta y cuatro

85. ochenta y cinco

86. ochenta y seis

87. ochenta y siete

88. ochenta y ocho

89. ochenta y nueve

90. **noventa**

91. noventa **y uno**

92. noventa y dos

93. noventa y tres

94. noventa y cuatro

95. noventa y cinco

96. noventa y seis

97. noventa y siete

98. noventa y ocho

99. noventa y nueve

100. **cien/ciento**

• No Y after ciento

⚠️ 100: cien
200: doscien<u>tos</u>

101. ciento uno

400. cuatrocien**tos**

903. novecien**tos** tres

1000. **mil**

• No Y after mil

1200. mil doscientos

3000. tres mil

2023. dos mil veintitrés

A	Let's practice!	**B**
43		120
55		300
61		16
74		501
37		190
21		105
86		7
32		12
85		450

Los días (los dee·yass)   - The days

≫ **Read and copy twice**

Monday
lunes
(loo·ness)

Tuesday
martes
(mahr·tess)

Wednesday
miércoles
(myehr·koh·less)

Thursday
jueves
(Hweh·bess)

_____

_____

Friday
viernes
(byehr·ness)

Saturday
sábado
(sah·bah·doh)

Sunday
domingo
(doh·meen·goh)

①

Unlike English, the days of the week and months in Spanish do not start with a capital letter.

_____

_____

El día
(el dee·yah)
- - - - - - - - -
The day

La semana
(la seh·mah·nah)
- - - - - - - - -
The week

El mes
(el mehs)
- - - - - - - - -
The month

El año
(el ah·nyoh)
- - - - - - - - -
The year

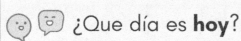 ¿Que día es **hoy**?   _What day is it **today**?_
(keh **dee**·ah ess oy)

≫ **Translate:** _Today is Monday._ ⇨ **Hoy es lunes.**

1. Today is Wednesday.

_ _ _ _ _ _ _ _ _ _ _ _ _ _

2. Today is Sunday.

_ _ _ _ _ _ _ _ _ _ _ _ _ _

3. Today is Tuesday.

4. Today is Thursday.

_ _ _ _ _ _ _ _ _ _ _ _ _ _

5. Today is Friday.

_ _ _ _ _ _ _ _ _ _ _ _ _ _

6. Today is Saturday.

≫ **Connect:**

Thursday •	• viernes
Sunday •	• jueves
Tuesday •	• domingo
Friday •	• lunes
Saturday •	• miércoles
Monday •	• martes
Wednesday •	• sábado

Los meses (los **meh**·sehs)   – The months

(Months are not capitalized in Spanish.)

>> **Read and copy twice.**

   enero (eh·**neh**·roh) JAN

  febrero (feh·**breh**·roh) FEB

 marzo (**mahr**·soh) MAR

  abril (ah·**breel**) APR

  mayo (**mah**·yoh) MAY

 junio (**Hoo**·nyoh) JUN

 julio (**Hoo**·lyoh) JUL

  agosto (ah·**gos**·toh) AUG

 septiembre (sehp·**tyem**·breh) SEP

 octubre (ok·**too**·breh) OCT

  noviembre (noh·**byem**·breh) NOV

  diciembre (dee·**syem**·breh) DEC

>> **Connect the months**

ABRIL •	January	July	• DICIEMBRE
MARZO •	February	August	• JULIO
MAYO •	March	September	• NOVIEMBRE
JUNIO •	April	October	• SEPTIEMBRE
ENERO •	May	November	• AGOSTO
FEBRERO •	June	December	• OCTUBRE

La fecha (la feh·chah)   – The date

There are a few differences to tell the date (*la fecha*) in Spanish:

⭐ The day comes before the month:

In the USA: In latin America / Spain

MONTH + DAY + YEAR .....becomes..... **DAY + MONTH + YEAR**

⭐ Add "**el**" before the day and "**de**" (deh) before the **month and year**.

flip

Examples: July 15, 2023 ....becomes........   15 **de** julio **de** 2023

So you can say: *Hoy es **el** lunes quince **de** julio **de** dos mil veintitrés*

⭐ The **1st** of the month is : "**primero**" in Spanish. • January **1st** = **primero** de enero

For 2nd and 3rd, use **dos**, **tres**... • January **2nd** = **dos** de enero

⭐ The date in numeric form is also reversed: **DAY / MONTH / YEAR**

November 7th: 7 de Noviembre:

In American   (11)/7/2004   In Spanish: 7/(11)/2004

English: ↘ The month is 1st   ↘ The month is 2nd place

≫ **Write the date in Spanish.**	≫ **Write the date in American English.**	≫**Switch to the Spanish forma**
Monday, <u>July 4</u>, 1999	Lunes 24 de febrero	01/25/2016
<u>August 14</u>, 2004	20 de marzo de 1980	11/13/1954
Tuesday, January 11	5 de octubre de 2013	08/07/2009
Saturday, October 14	Miércoles 6 de mayo de 2021	02/21/2022
December 25, 2008	Viernes 11 de junio	05/14/2024

- Pronouns -

Yo (yoh)

I

Tú (too) **Usted** (oos·ted)

you

- <u>Tú</u>: Informal Use with friends & family...
- <u>Usted</u>: Formal Polite

ÉL (el)

He

Ella (eh·yah)

She

Nosotros (noh·soh·trohs)

We

(oos·teh·dess)

Ustedes

you

- For 2 or more people
- In Spain, use
  - vosotros (m.)
  - vosotras (f.)

(eh·yohs)

Ellos

They

- Use for 2 or more **male**
- Or group of 2 or more **mixed** gender (male + fem.)

(eh·yass)

Ellas

They

- For a group of 2 or more **female only.**

Read outloud and write four times.

Yo ___ ___   **Nosotros** ___ ___

Tú ___ ___   **Ustedes** ___ ___

Usted ___ ___   **Ellos** ___ ___

Ella ___ ___   **Ellas** ___ ___

Él ___ ___

Shortcuts:
(for.) Formal   (mix.) Mixed gender
(inf.) Informal (m.) Male:
(pl.) Plural   (f.) Female
                 (sing.) Singular

Important:

• *Tú* is informal/familiar. Use with *friends* and *family*.

• *Usted* is used when speaking to 1 person in formal (for.)/polite speech (like a teacher, an adult person you don't know well or to show respect...)

• Some countries (Argentina...) use **vos** instead of **tú**.

• In Spain, *Ustedes* is **vosotros/as**. (boh·**soh**·trohs/ahs)

• *Ellos* refers to a group of 2 or more male or mixed group (even if there is only 1 male and several females).

(Connect the pronouns)

He •	Yo	Usted	• They (m. / mix.)
I •	Tú	Nosotros	• They (f.)
You (inf.)•	Usted	Ustedes	• You (for.)
She •	Él	Ellas	• You (pl.)
You (for.) •	Ella	Ellos	• We (for.)

≫ Write the correct pronouns.

I

....

You (inf.)

....

You (for.)

....

He

....

She

....

We

....

You (pl.)

....

They (m.)

....

They (mix.)

....

They (f.)

....

SER / ESTAR (sair /ehs•tahr) — To be

Let's move on to the verb "To be". This verb can confuse Spanish learners as there are actually 2 ways to express "to be" in Spanish: **Ser** and **Estar**.
Let's start with Ser. Ser describes permanent (or long-lasting) characteristics:

SER (sehr) — To be

- Yo soy — I am
- Tú eres — You are (sing.) (inf.)
- Él es — He is
- Ella es — She is
- Usted es — You are (sing.) (for.)
- Nosotros somos — We are
- Ellos son — They are (m.) (mix.)
- Ellas son — They are (f.)
- Ustedes son — You are (pl.)

1. **Description:** *(Physical/permanent character.)*
   La flor es roja.   *The flower is red.*

2. **Profession:** Yo soy estudiante.   *I am a student.*

3. **Origin /Nationality/ Identification:**
   Pedro es mexicano.   *Pedro is Mexican.*
   Pedro es **de** Mexico.   *Pedro is **from** Mexico.*

4. **Material:** La mesa es **de** plástico.
   *The table is **of** plastic.*

5. **Before nouns:** Es un libro.   *It's a book.*

6. **Ownership/Possession:** + use of **de** (of)
   El libro es de María.   *The book is María's.*

7. **Event Location:** La fiesta es en mi casa.
   The party is at my house.

≫ Translate and write twice.

He is _____

You are (sing./ inf.) _____

I am _____

She is _____

They are (m.) _____

You are (sing./ for.) _____

They are (f.) _____

You are (pl.) _____

We are _____

- The abbreviation of Usted is **Ud.**
- The abbreviation of Ustedes is **Uds.**
- *You are* (pl.) in Spain is **vosotros sois**
- **Ser** is also used to tell the time, prices...

Connect.

You are (pl.)	Ud. es	Ella es	He is
They are (m.)	Uds. son	Tú eres	I am
We are	Ella es	Él es	She is
You are (Sing., for.)	Ellos son	Yo soy	You are (Sing., inf.)
She is	Nosotros somos		

Complete with the correct form of SER and indicate which concept is expressed:

- **Description** - **Origin** - **Before nouns** - **Event Location**
- **Profession** - **Material** - **Ownership**

Ex: Pedro ___es___ mi hermano. _identification_   *Pedro is my brother.*

1. Él _____ doctor. ....   *He is a doctor.*

2. ¿Tú _____ de California? ....   *You are from California?*

3. Las niñas _____ simpáticas. ....   *The girls are nice.*

4. La casa _____ de madera. ....   *The house is (made) of wood.*

5. El carro _____ de mi padre. ....   *The car is my father's.*

6. Carlos y yo _____ americanos. .....   *Carlos and I are Americans.*

7. El concierto _____ en Los Ángeles. ...   *The concert is in Los Angeles.*

8. _____ un carro. ....   *It's a car.*

9. Ella _____ mi hermana. ....   *She is my sister.*

10. Yo _____ de Colombia. ....   *I am from Colombia.*

11. Mi madre _____ maestra. ....   *My mother is a teacher.*

12. Mis zapatos _____ de cuero. ......   *My shoes are (made) of leather.*

13. Tu hermano _____ muy alto. ....   *You brother is very tall.*

(!) Remember: In general, Ser is used for permanent or long lasting characteristics.

Ser has many other uses, We will study those in level 2.

*Let's now learn about the other verb to say "to be": **Estar**.*

ESTAR — To be
(es·**tahr**)

- Yo estoy — I am
- Tú estás — You are (sing.) (inf.)
- Él está — He is
- Ella está — She is
- Ud. está — You are (sing.) (for.)
- Nosotros estamos — We are
- Ellos están — They are (m.) (mix.)
- Ellas están — They are (f.)
- Uds. están* — You are (pl.)

*In general, **estar** describes more temporary concepts such as:*

1. **Location:** (of **people** and **things**)

   Estamos en la casa. *We are in the house.*

2. **Health:**

   ¿Estás enfermo? *Are you sick?*

3. **Opinion:** (about appearance or taste)

   ¡La comida está rica! *The food is delicious!*

   ¡Ana está guapa hoy! *Ana is beautiful today!*

4. **Mood/Emotion/Condition:**

   Estoy cansado. *I am tired.*

* ***You are** (pl.) with "estar" in Spain is **vosotros estáis.***   (boh·**soh**·trohs es·**tah**·ees)

>> Translate and write twice. (Use the abbreviations for *usted* and *ustedes*.)

She is

He is

You are
(sing./ inf.)

I am

You are
(sing./ for.)

They are
(f.)

You are
(pl.)

We are

They are
(m.)

(!) **Remember**: In general, estar is used for temporary concepts.

A Complete with the correct form of ESTAR and indicate which concept is expressed:

1. La sopa _____ buena. _____ *The soup is good.*
2. Los niños _____ feliz hoy. _____ *The children are happy today.*
3. Mi padre _____ enfermo. _____ *My father is sick.*
4. (Yo) _____ en mi casa. _____ *I am in my house.*
5. Mi amiga _____ triste hoy. _____ *My friend is sad today.*
6. La comida _____ sabrosa. _____ *The food is delicious.*
7. Tu teléfono _____ en la mesa. _____ *Your phone is on the table.*
8. La niña _____ feliz. _____ *The girl is happy.*
9. ¿(Tú) _____ listo? _____ *Are you ready?*
10. Mi amigo _____ en el hospital. _____ *My friend is in the hospital.*
11. (Nosotros) _____ en la playa. _____ *We are at the beach.*

(!) Pronouns (yo, tú...) are often omitted because the verb ending /and context indicate who the subject is. The pronouns in parenthesis above are not necessary.

SER

1. Description
2. Profession
3. Origin /Nationality/ Identification
4. Material
5. Before nouns
6. Ownership
7. Event Location

ESTAR

1. Location *(People & things)*
2. Health
3. Opinion
4. Mood/condition...

B **Ser or Estar? Which verb would you use:**

Ex: Your house is beautiful. ser   *Ex: He's at home.* estar

1. This **is** my cousin. _____
2. **I am** sick today. _____
3. This book **is** interesting. _____
4. She **is** Mexican. _____
5. My sister **is** a nurse. _____
6. **Are** you upset? _____
7. This **is** my dog. _____
8. He **is** catholic. _____
9. It**'s** a cake. _____
10. **I'm** at work. _____

- Greetings -

There are two ways to speak with someone in Spanish: **informally** (with friends, family, children...) or **formally** with grown-ups like a teacher, strangers, waiters...)

Recipe to introduce yourself:

STEP 1 : Pick a greeting

¡Hola!
(oh·lah)

!Buenos días!
(bweh·nohs dee·ahs)

!Buenas tardes!
(bweh·nahs tar·dehs)

Means **Hello!** or **Hi!** .Most common. Can be used alongside other greetings.

Means **Good morning** *or* **Good day.**

Similar to **Good evening**. Can be used until the sun goes down.

STEP 2: Ask "how are you?"

Informal/friendly

¿Cómo estás?

(koh·moh ehs·tahs)

Formal/polite speech

¿Cómo está usted?

(koh·moh ehs·tah oos·ted)

>> **Choose the correct greeting from step 1 and 2:**

A
_____

_____

B
_____

_____

C
_____

_____

A How would you say "*How are you?*" to:

1. your friend: _____

2. your teacher: _____

3. an older person: _____

4. a child: _____

(!) To say **How are you (all)?** to a group, say: **¿Cómo están?**

STEP 3 : To say that you're doing well:

Estoy bien, gracias

(ess•**toy** byen **grahs**•yahs)

I'm doing well, thank you

Muy bien, gracias

(mwee byen **grahs**•yahs)

Very well, thank you

(You can also just say "Bien, gracias")

STEP 4 : Ask "And you?"

Informal speech

¿Y tú?

(ee too)

Formal

¿Y usted?

(ee oos•**ted**)

B Translate:

1. Good morning. How are you? (for.) _____

2. Very well, thank you. And you? (for.) _____

3. Hi! How are you? (inf.) _____

4. Well (good), thanks. And you? (inf.) _____

5. Good evening! How are you? (pl.) _____

≫ **Read several times to practice:**

¡Hola!

- ¡Hola! ¿Cómo estás?
- Muy bien, gracias. ¿Y tú?
- Bien, gracias.

¡Buenos días!

- ¡Buenos días!
- Estoy bien, gracias. ¿Y usted?
- Muy bien, gracias.

• If you don't feel too well, you could reply instead: (copy twice)

No tan bien ------------------

(noh tahn byen)

Not very well ------------------

Mal ------------------

(mahl)

Bad ------------------

STEP 5 : Ask: "What's your name?"

Informal

¿Cómo te llamas?

(**koh**•moh teh **yah**•mas)

Formal

¿Cómo se llama usted?

(**koh**•moh seh **yah**•mah **oos**•ted)

STEP 6 : Say "My name is..."

Me llamo ... (+ name)

(meh **yah**•moh ...)

Me llamo Frank

STEP 7 : Ask " How old are you?"

Literally: How many years do you "have"?

Informal

¿Cuántos años tienes?

(kwan·tohs ahn·yos tyeh·nehs)

Formal

¿Cuántos años tiene?

(kwan·tohs ahn·yos tyeh·neh)

STEP 8 : Say: "I'm ... years old"

Tengo ... (number) años

(tehn·goh ... ahn·yos)

"Tengo" means "I have"
I'm 13 : Tengo trece años

STEP 9 : Say Goodbye, see you later...

¡Adios!

(ah·dyohs)
Goodbye!

¡Hasta luego!

(ahs·tah lweh·goh)
See you later!

¡Nos vemos!

(nos beh·mohs)
See you!

≫ **Let's review, translate these sentences:** *Add ¡ or ¿ (see p.62)*

1. How old are you? (inf.) _____

2. Hi! What's your name? (inf.) _____

3. My name is ... _____

4. I'm 16 years old. _____

5. What's your name? (for.) _____

6. How old are you? (for.) _____

7. I'm 20 years old? _____

8. Goodbye! See you! _____

9. See you later! _____

>> Let see it in action! Read:

¡Hola!

¡Buenos días!

- ¡Hola! Cómo estás?
- Estoy bien gracias. ¿Y tú?
- Muy bien, gracias.
- Cómo te llamas?
- Me llamo Marc. ¿Y tú?
- Me llamo Adam.
- ¿Cuántos años tienes?
- Tengo doce años.

- ¡Buenos días! ¿Cómo está usted?
- Muy bien, gracias. ¿Y usted?
- Estoy bien, gracias.
- ¿Cómo se llama usted?
- Me llamo Maria. ¿Y usted?
- Me llamo Tina.
- ¿Cuántos años tiene?
- Tengo treinta años.

>> Fill in the blanks:

- !Hola! Me _____ Lisa. ¿Cómo te _____?
- ___ llamo Adam. ¿ _____ estás?
- Muy _____ , gracias. ¿Y ____ ?
- _____ muy bien, gracias.

> Talking to a group or Asking about people (pl.):
>
> "¿Cómo están?"
> "¿Cómo se llaman?"
> "¿Cuántos años tienen?"

>> Fill in the blanks:

- _____ días *Señora**López! Cómo _____ usted hoy?
- _____ muy bien, gracias señor* García.
Y _____ ?
- _____ bien, _____ !

> * **Señora:** Madam/ Mrs
> (seh•**nyoh**•rah)
> **Señor:** Mister/ Sir
> (seh•**nyor**)
> **Hoy:** Today (oy)

28

- Articles -

In Spanish, nouns (people, places, things, idea...) have a gender: they are either feminine or masculine. **Articles** are words like **the** or **a/an**.
There are a few more articles in Spanish than in English because the articles change to agree with the gender and number of the nouns (singular/plural).

Remember that:
- Most nouns ending in **-o** are masculine
- Most nouns ending in **-a** are feminine

THE :

• El (el)	with masculine nouns	**El niño** (el **nee**•nyoh)	*The boy*
• La (lah)	with feminine nouns	**La niña** (lah **nee**•nyah)	*The girl*
• Los (lohs)	with masculine plural nouns	**Los niños** (lohs **nee**•nyohs)	*The boys*
• Las (lahs)	with feminine plural nouns	**Las niñas** (lahs **nee**•nyahs)	*The girls*

A/An:

Un (oon)	with masculine nouns	**Un niño** (oon **nee**•nyoh)	*A boy*
Una (oo•nah)	with feminine nouns	**Una niña** (oo•nah **nee**•nyah)	*A girl*

Some

Unos (oo•nohs)	with masc. plural nouns	**Unos niños**	*Some boys*
Unas (oo•nahs)	with fem. plural nouns	**Unas niñas**	*Some girls*

 *Spanish is a rich language with many synonyms. There are often several ways to say the same thing. (ex: **bedroom** = el cuarto, la habitación, la recámara...)*

La familia (lah fah•**mee**•lyah) — The family

>> **Read outloud and write twice.**

La familia
(fah•**mee**•lyah)

_____

_____

El padre
(**pah**•dreh)

_____

_____

La madre
(**mah**•dreh)

_____

_____

El hermano
(ehr•**mah**•noh)

_____

_____

La hermana
(ehr•**mah**•nah)

_____

_____

El abuelo
(ah•**bweh**•loh)

_____

_____

La abuela
(ah•**bweh**•lah)

_____

_____

El tío
(**tee**•oh)

_____

_____

La tía
(**tee**•ah)

_____

_____

Connect the words.

The brother •	El tío
The mother •	La hermana
The sister •	El abuelo
The uncle •	El hermano
The grandfather •	La madre
The aunt •	La familia
The grandmother •	El padre
The father •	La tía
The family •	La abuela

Choose the correct article.

- La o El famillia
- La o El tío
- La o El hermano
- La o El madre
- La o El padre

- La o El abuela
- La o El abuelo
- La o El tía
- La o El hermana

Also:
Mom is mamá
Dad is papá

"o"(oh) **means "or"**

Translate. *(Try to translate from memory.)*

The family _____

The grandfather _____

The brother _____

The mother _____

The grandmother _____

The uncle _____

The father _____

The aunt _____

The sister _____

≫ **Read outloud and write twice.**

La casa
(**kah**·sah)

_____

_____

La cocina
(koh·**see**·nah)

_____

_____

La sala
(**sah**·lah)

_____

_____

La habitación
(ah·bee·tah·**syohn**)

Also: el cuarto

_____

_____

El baño
(**bah**·nyoh)

_____

_____

El inodoro
(ee·noh·**doh**·roh)

_____

_____

El jardín (Hahr·**deen**)

_____

_____

La cochera
(koh·**cheh**·rah)   Also: el garaje

_____

_____

Las escaleras
(es·kah·**leh**·rahs)

_____

_____

» Connect the words.

The restrooms •	La cocina
The living room •	La cochera
The garage •	Las escaleras
The house •	El jardín
The bathroom •	El inodoro
The stairs •	La habitación
The backyard •	La sala
The kitchen •	La casa
The bedroom •	El baño

» Circle the correct article.

"o" (oh) **means "or"**

- La ○ El sala
- La ○ El inodoro
- La ○ El baño
- La ○ El cocina

- La ○ El cochera
- La ○ El habitación
- Las ○ Los escaleras
- La ○ El jardín
- La ○ El casa

» Translate

The bathroom	The house	The backyard
The living room	The garage	The restrooms
The kitchen	The bedroom	The stairs

SENTENCE BUILDER *- Possessives (Part 1)*

Time to put all this new vocabulary together and start building simple sentences. But first, let's learn how to say "**my**" and "**your**" (inf.).

- with singular nouns: -   with plural nouns:

My: **Mi** (mee)   **Mis** (mees)

My brother = Mi hermano
My brothers = Mi**s** hermano**s**

Your: **Tu** (too)   **Tus** (toos)

Your brother = Tu hermano
Your brothers = Tu**s** hermano**s**

*No accent on **tu**. This is the informal "your". You can use it with anyone you are on familiar term with (friends and family, kids...).*

≫ **Translate:** *(Here, plural nouns take an -s)*

Vocabulary:
in: **en** (ehn)
and: **y** (ee)
with: **con** (kon)

1. My family is in the living room.

_____

2. My aunts are in the bedroom.

_____

3. My mother is in the kitchen with your sisters.

_____

4. They (m.) are in the garage with my father and your brothers.

_____

5. I am in my bedroom with my sisters and my grandmother.

_____

6. Your grandfather and my uncle are in your house.

_____

7. We are in the backyard with your family.

_____

*Did you remember to use **estar** since we're describing the **location of people**? Great!*

≫ **Read outloud and write twice.**

El sillón
(see•**yohn**)

_____

_____

El refrigerador
(rreh•free•Heh•rah•**dohr**)

_____

_____

La silla
(see•yah)

_____

_____

La ventana
(behn•**tah**•nah)

_____

_____

La puerta
(**pwehr**•tah)

_____

_____

La cama
(**kah**•mah)

_____

_____

El teléfono
(teh•**leh**•foh•noh)

_____

_____

La televisión
(teh•leh•bee•**syon**)

Also: tele

_____

_____

La computadora
(kom•poo•tah•**do**•rah)

_____

_____

35

>> Connect the words.

The tv •	El sillón
The chair •	La computadora
The phone •	La televisión
The fridge •	La puerta
The sofa •	La cama
The computer •	La ventana
The window •	El teléfono
The bed •	La silla
The door •	El refrigerador

A Circle the correct article.

- La o El   computadora
- La o El   silla
- La o El   ventana
- La o El   televisión

- La o El   sillón
- La o El   puerta
- La o El   refrigerador
- La o El   teléfono
- La o El   cama

B Translate *(Try to translate from memory.)*

My tv	Your chairs	My door
Your sillón	My windows	Your phone
My bed	Your computer	My fridge

>> **Read outloud and write twice.**

El salón de clase
(sah·**lohn** deh **klah**·seh)

Also: el aula

_____

_____

El profesor
(proh·feh·**sohr**)

_____

_____

El escritorio
(es·kree·**toh**·ryoh)

_____

_____

La tarea
(tah·**reh**·ah)

Homework:
Do ALL
exercises
Page 28 to 30

_____

_____

El libro
(**lee**·broh)

_____

_____

El cuaderno
(kwah·**dehr**·noh)

_____

_____

La lapicera
(lah·pee·**seh**·rah)

Spain: el boli

_____

_____

El lápiz
(lah·pees)

_____

_____

El estudiante
(ess·too·**dyahn**·teh)

_____

_____

Connect the words.

The teacher •	El escritorio
The book •	El salón de clase
The pencil •	El libro
The desk •	La lapicera
The student •	El profesor
The notebook •	La tarea
The classroom •	El lápiz
The homework •	El cuaderno
The pen •	El estudiante

Circle the correct article.

• La ○ El lápiz   • La ○ El lapicera

• La ○ El cuaderno   • La ○ El tarea

• La ○ El libro   • La ○ El escritorio

• La ○ El salón de clase • La ○ El profesor

! • *El* profesor: male teacher (m), *La* profesor**a** : female teacher (f).

• *El* estudiante: male student, **La** estudiante : female student.

Translate. *(Try to translate from memory.)*

Your pencil	Your desk	The student (fem.)
Your teacher (fem.)	My homework	My notebook<u>s</u>
Your book<u>s</u>	My pens	My classroom

Let's now learn some more possessive adjectives: **your** (form.)/(pl), **our, their**...
Nuestr**o** (our) becomes nuestr**a** with a feminine noun. Add an **-s** for plurals.

	with singular nouns:	with plural nouns:	
Your: -use with: • group of 2 or more • 1 person **formally**	**Su** (soo)	**Sus** (soos)	*Your book:* Su libro *Your books* = Sus libros
Our:	**Nuestro/a** (nwehs•troh/ah)	**Nuestros/as** (nwehs•trohs/ahs)	*Our house:* Nuestra casa *Our books:* Nuestros libro
His/Her/ Their:	**Su** (soo)	**Sus** (soos)	*Her/His/Their book:* Su libro *Their books* = Sus libros

(!) In spain, **Your** (informal/plural) is **vuestro**(s)/**a**(s). *(your house: vuestra casa)*

A Circle the correct possessive.

- su   o   sus   cama
- tu   o   tus   teléfono
- su   o   sus   profesores
-   mis   o   mi   madre

- nuestros   o   nuestra   cuadernos
- nuestro   o   nuestra   profesora
- nuestro   o   nuestra   sillón
- nuestros   o   nuestras   lapiceras

Singular   plural.

Remember: mi/tu/su/nuestro/a — mis/tus/sus/nuestros/as

B Translate. (For "your", use the one used formally/for a group)

His father	Our bed	Your sisters
_____	_____	_____
Our teacher (f.)	His bedroom	Her house
_____	_____	_____
Your books	Our brothers	Their mother
_____	_____	_____

- More people -

>> **Read outloud then write twice.**

El amigo
(ah•**mee**•goh)

friend (m.)

_____

_____

La amiga
(ah•**mee**•gah)

friend (f.)

_____

_____

El primo
(**pree**•moh)

cousin
(m.)

_____

_____

La prima
(**pree**•mah)

cousin (f.)

_____

_____

La persona
(pehr•**soh**•nah)

person

_____

_____

La gente   people
(**Hen**•teh)

_____

_____

(!) *2 people ..: **dos personas ...***

>> **Translate**. *(Try to translate from memory.)*

My friend (f.)	My friends (m./pl)	My cousin (f.)
Your friends (inf./m.)	(the) People	The person
Three people	My cousins (f./pl)	Her friend (f.)
His cousins (m.)	Their friends	Our cousins (mix)

SENTENCE BUILDER

Time to put all you have learned together and build more sentences.
Do your best to use your memory, if you can not remember, it's ok to go back and search for these words.

≫ **Translate**.

1. My <u>friends</u> are in my bedroom. (m.)

---

2. Her brother is with our <u>cousins</u> in the garage. (mix.)

---

3. My father is in the living room with my mother.

---

4. Today, I am at school with my <u>friends</u>. (m.) (think: **in the** school)

---

5. His sisters are in the backyard with my grandmother.

---

6. Lisa is in the kitchen with her friends. (f.)

---

7. My name is Maria and I am a student. (no need to put "a")

---

8. The students are in the classroom with their <u>teacher</u>. (f.)

---

9. Your computer and your books are in my bedroom. (form.)

---

10. My uncle and my aunt are in their house with my cousins.

TENER (teh·nehr) — To have

Now that you have mastered **Ser y Estar** (right?) Let's move on to another important verb: Tener (teh·nehr) "To have".

I have	(Yo)	**Tengo** (ten·goh)
You have	(Tú)	**Tienes** (tyeh·nehs)
He/She/It has	(Él /Ella)	**Tiene** (tyeh·neh)
You have (form.)	(Ud.)	
We have	(nosotros)	**Tenemos** (teh·neh·mos)
You have (pl.)	(Uds.)	**Tienen** (tyeh·nen)
They have	(Ellos /Ellas)	**Tienen** (tyeh·nen)

(!) In Spain, **You have** (inf./plural) is **vosotros tenéis**).

≫ <u>Translate and write twice.</u> (Use the abbreviations for *usted* and *ustedes*.)

She has _____

He has _____

You have
(sing./ inf.) _____

I have _____

You have
(sing./ for.) _____

They have
(f.) _____

You have
(pl.) _____

We have _____

They have
(m.) _____

 Oftentimes, subject pronouns (Yo, tú...) are omitted since the verb or the context shows who or what the subject is. They can still be used to clarify the subject or for emphasis.

Uds. tienen	• He has	Ellas tienen	• It has
Él tiene	• You have (pl.)	Tienes	• She has
Tenemos	• You have (sing./ form.)	Ella tiene	• I have
Ellos tienen	• We have	Tiene	• They have (f.)
Ud. tiene	•They have (m.)	Tengo	• You have (inf.)

>> **Complete with the verb "tener".**

1. (Él) _____ une casa grande.

2. Ellos _____ un carro. (a car)

3. Ellas _____ un teléfono.

4. Ud. _____ una televisión.

5. Tú _____ una computadora en tu habitación.

6. Yo _____ dos hermanos.

7. Uds. _____ una grande familia.

8. Nosotros _____ amigos.

9. Mis primos_____ un jardín en su casa.

10. Yo _____ un teléfono.

>> **Connect.**

Yo •	tienes
Ella •	tiene
Tú •	tienen
Él •	tengo
Uds. •	tiene

Ud. •	tienen
Nosotros •	tiene
Ellos •	tienen
Ellas •	tenemos

El cuerpo (el **kwehr**•poh)   – The body

>> <u>**Read outloud and write twice.**</u>

La cabeza
(kah•**beh**•sah)

Los ojos
(oh•Hos)

La nariz
(nah•rees)

_____

_____

La boca
(**boh**•kah)

El estómago
(es•**toh**•mah•go)

El brazo
(**brah**•soh)

_____

_____

La mano
(**mah**•noh)

La pierna
(**pyehr**•nah)

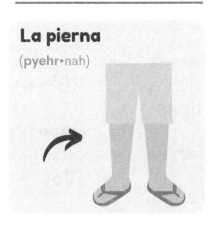

El pie
(pyeh)

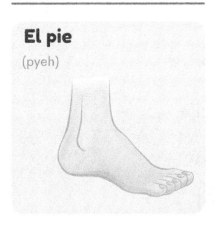

_____

_____

The legs •	Los ojos
The head •	La boca
The feet •	Las piernas
The nose •	Los brasos
The arms •	Las manos
The hands •	El estómago
The eyes •	La nariz
The stomach •	La cabeza
The mouth •	Los pies

A <u>Circle the correct article.</u>

• La ○ El mano
• La ○ El estómago
• La ○ El nariz

• Las ○ Los ojos
• Las ○ Los piernas
• Los ○ Las brasos

• La ○ El cuerpo
• La ○ El cabeza
• La ○ El boca
• La ○ El pie

B <u>Translate</u>.

Their feet	Your head (inf.)	Her arm
_____	_____	_____
Your nose (inf.)	His mouth	Your leg (form.)
_____	_____	_____
My eyes	My stomach	Our hands
_____	_____	_____
<u>Remember:</u>		My body
The body = El cuerpo		_____

45

La enfermedad (lah ehn·fehr·meh·dad) – Sickness

Now that you know many body parts, let's learn how to say that **something hurt**:

DOLER + body part
- becomes **duele + sing. / duelen + pl.**

• **my** ... hurt	→ **me** duele ...	
• **your** (inf.) ... hurt	→ **te** duele ...	"the"
• **his/her/your** (for.)... hurt	→ **le** duele ...	**+** body
• **our** ... hurt	→ **nos** duele ...	part name
• **their/your** (pl.) ... hurt	→ **les** duele ...	

• **Me/te/se... duele el/la** + singular

Me duel**e la** cabeza: *I have a headache*
(dweh·leh)   *(My head hurts)*

• **Me/te/se... duele**n **los/las** + plural

Te duele**n las** pierna**s**: *Your legs hurt*
(dweh·lehn)

• I have fever: **Tengo fiebre** (fyeh·breh)

• You have a cold: **Tienes un resfriado**
(rehs·fryah·doh)

• To be sick is: **Estar enfermo/a**
(ehn·fehr·moh)

- I am sick: Estoy enfermo/enferma (f.)

≫ Translate.

1. She has a headache/Her head hurts.

_____

2. I have a stomachache today.

_____

3. I am sick, I have a cold.

_____

4. We are sick, we have fever.

_____

5. My eyes hurt.

_____

6. My father is sick, he has a headache.

_____

7. Your hand hurt. (your: inf.)

_____

8. You have a stomachache, you are sick. (you: for.)

_____

9. He is sick. He has fever and he has a cold.

_____

Los colores (los koh·loh·rehs) — Colors

>> **Color the shapes then write twice, remember to read outloud.**

Azul   Blue
(ah·**sool**)

Blanco   White
(**blahn**·koh)

Rojo   Red
(roh·Hoh)

Negro   Black
(**neh**·groh)

Verde   Green
(**behr**·deh)

Amarillo   Yellow
(ah·mah·**ree**·yoh)

Anaranjado   Orange
(ah·nah·rahn·**Hah**·doh)

Marrón   Brown
(mah·**rrohn**)

Rosado   Pink
(roh·**sah**·doh)

also: naranja

also: café

also: rosa

⟫ Connect the words.

Red •	Anaranjado
Orange •	Blanco
Black •	Marrón/Café
Yellow •	Azul
Brown •	Rojo
White •	Rosado/Rosa
Pink •	Verde
Blue •	Amarillo
Green •	Negro

⟫ **When colors are used as adjectives they must agree with the noun they modify in number and gender:**

masculine	feminine	plural/masc.	plural/fem.
Blanco	Blanca	Blancos	Blancas
Rojo	Roja	Rojos	Rojas
Negro	Negra	Negros	Negras

- Only **colores** ending in **-o** change to **-a** in the feminine. <u>Other colors don't change</u>
- All colors take an **-s** in the plural, or **-es** if they end in a consonant. (azul – azules)

⟫ Translate.

Red (m./pl.)   Blue (m./sing.)   Orange (f./pl.)

_____   _____   _____

Green (m./pl.)   Black (f./sing)   Yellow (m./sing.)

_____   _____   _____

White (f./pl.)   Pink (m./pl.)   Brown (f./sing)

_____   _____   _____

SENTENCE BUILDER

You've learned quite a few words, including 3 of the most important verbs in the present tense. *"Practice makes perfect"* so let's practice!

For plurals, remember to add -**s** or -**es** in words ending in a consonant.

>> **Translate**.

1. I have two legs and two hands.

_____

2. <u>Your</u> eyes are green. (for.)

_____

3. <u>You</u> have a yellow kitchen. (inf.)

_____

4. My house is brown and white.

_____

5. Her bed is blue but her room is pink.

_____

> **Colors can be adjectives**
>
> • Adjectives are words that describe things.
>
> • Colors in Spanish come **after** the noun.
>
> Ex: <u>blue</u> books = libros <u>azules</u>

6. We have two red books and three green pens.

_____

7. My computer and my notebook are in <u>your</u> bedroom. (inf.)

_____

8. My mouth and my nose hurt.

_____

9. My sister has blue eyes.

_____

10. I have a black desk but my chair is red.

_____

> **Vocabulary:**
> **but:** pero
> (peh·roh)
> **today:** Hoy
> (oy)

>> **Read outloud and write twice.**

El abrigo
(ah·**bree**·goh)

_____

_____

Los pantalones
(pan·tah·**loh**·ness)

_____

_____

La camiseta
(kah·mee·**seh**·tah)

_____

_____

El vestido
(behs·**tee**·doh)

_____

_____

La falda
(**fahl**·dah)

_____

_____

El pijama
(pee·**yah**·mah)

_____

_____

La ropa interior
(**roh**·pah een·teh·**ryohr**)

underwear

_____

_____

Los calcetines
(kahl·seh·**tee**·nehs)

_____

_____

Los zapatos
(sah·**pah**·tohs)

_____

_____

Connect the words.

The t-shirt •	El pijama
The dress •	Los pantalónes
The shoes •	El abrigo
The pants •	El vestido
The underwear •	Los calcetines
The pjs •	Los zapatos
The socks •	La camiseta
The coat •	La falda
The skirt •	La ropa interior

» **Circle the correct article.**

• La ○ El falda
• La ○ El camiseta
• La ○ El abrigo
• La ○ El pijama

• Las ○ Los pantalones
• La ○ El vestido
• La ○ El ropa interior
• Las ○ Los calcetines
• Las ○ Los zapatos

Note: The sweater is "el suéter" in Spanish and the jacket is "la chaqueta". Easy to remember!   (sweh·tehr)   (chah·keh·tah)

» **Translate.**

The socks	The dress	The skirt
The underwear	The shoes	The pants
The pajamas	The t-shirt	The coat

>> **Read outloud then write twice.**

Un hombre
(**ohm**•breh)

_____

_____

Una mujer
(moo•**Hehr**•)

_____

_____

Los niños
(nee•nyohs)

_____

_____

Un niño
(nee•nyoh)

_____

_____

Una niña
(nee•nyah)

_____

_____

El bebé
(beh•beh)

_____

_____

El desayuno   breakfast
(deh•sah•**yoo**•noh)

_____

_____

El almuerzo   lunch
(ahl•**mwehr**•soh)

_____

_____

La cena   dinner
(**seh**•nah)

_____

_____

Connect the words.

The man •	El desayuno
The woman •	El niño
The children •	El bebé
The boy •	La cena
The girl •	La niña
The baby •	La mujer
The breakfast •	El almuerzo
The lunch •	El hombre
The dinner •	Los niños

Circle the correct article.

- La o El niña
- La o El cena
- La o El niño
- La o El mujer

- La o El almuerzo
- La o El hombre
- La o El desayuno
- La o Los niños

Note: A baby boy is **un bebé** (m.), a baby girl is **una bebé** (f.)

Translate. Some are in the plural form: use **los** (masc.) or **las** (fem.)

The babies	The boys	The men
The breakfast	The dinner	The lunch
The women	The girls	The children

Add -s for plurals, or -es if the noun ends in a consonant. (profesor - profesores)

SENTENCE BUILDER

Time for more practice. Here's some new words:

- It's: **Es** (ess)

- Come here!: **¡Ven aquí!**
  → *to 1 person* (ben ah•kee)

- Come here!: **¡Vengan aquí!**
  → *to a group* (ben•gahn ah•kee)

- It's { -breakfast / -lunch / -dinner } time!: **Es hora** { **del desayuno** / **del almuerzo** / **de cenar** }
  (ess **oh**•rah)

- It's time to eat!: **¡Es hora de comer!**
  (ess oh•rah deh koh•mehr)

1. The girl has a yellow dress.   Remember: <u>colors</u> come <u>after</u> the noun.

_____

2. The woman has a baby, it's a boy.

_____

3. It's breakfast time! Come here! *(to 1 person)*

_____

4. The kids have blue shoes.

_____

5. His pants are black pero his coat is white.

_____

6. It's lunch time. Come here, it's time to eat! *(to a group)*

_____

7. Her family has a brown house and a red car.

_____

8. It's dinner time. Come here! *(to 1 person)*

_____

9. I have a headache today. *(i.e. :my head hurts)*

_____

10. My brother is sick, he has a stomachache.

_____

La mesa (lah **meh**·sah) — The table

>> <u>**Read outloud then write twice.**</u>

El plato
(**plah**·toh)

_____

_____

El tenedor
(teh·neh·**dohr**)

_____

_____

El cuchillo
(koo·**chee**·yoh)

_____

_____

La cuchara
(koo·**chah**·rah)

_____

_____

El vaso
(**bah**·soh)

_____

_____

La servilleta
(sehr·bee·**yeh**·tah)

_____

_____

La comida
(koh·**mee**·dah)

Food

_____

_____

La cacerola
(kah·seh·**roh**·lah)

_____

_____

La botella
(boh·**teh**·yah)

_____

_____

55

Fill in the blanks with the correct name.

Circle the correct article.

- El o La   tenedor
- El o La   comida
- El o La   plato
- El o La   cacerola

- El o La   botella
- El o La   vaso
- El o La   servilleta
- El o La   cuchillo
- El o La   cuchara

Translate.

The glass/cup	The napkin	The saucepan
The fork	The knife	The spoon
The food	The bottle	The plate

La comida

>> **Read outloud then write twice.**

El pan
(pan)

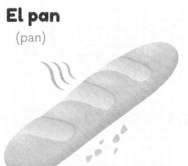

_____

_____

Los huevos
(**weh**·bohs)

_____

_____

La carne
(**kahr**·neh)

_____

_____

El pollo
(**poh**·yoh)

_____

_____

El pescado
(pehs·**kah**·doh)

_____

_____

El arroz
(ah·**rrohs**)

_____

_____

La pasta
(**pahs**·tah)

_____

_____

La leche
(**leh**·cheh)

_____

_____

El agua
(**ah**·gwah)

_____

_____

Connect the words.

The fish •   El agua

The water •   El pescado

The bread •   El pollo

The eggs •   La pasta

The chicken •   Los huevos

The milk •   La carne

The meat •   La leche

The pasta •   El arroz

The rice •   El pan

Circle the correct article.

- El   o   La   pan
- El   o   La   carne
- El   o   La   leche
- El   o   La   pescado

- El   o   La   arroz
- El   o   La   pollo
- El   o   La   pasta
- El   o   La   agua
- El   o   La   huevo

(!) "**Pescado**" is the culinary term for fish. The animal is: **el pez/los peces**
(fishes)(peh•sehs)

Translate.

The fish (food)	The milk	The chicken
The water	The eggs	The rice
The pasta	The meat	The bread

Articles (Part 2)

So far, we have only used **the**: **el/la/los/las.** These are *definite articles.*
We now need to learn how to use a/an (indefinite articles) and *some.*

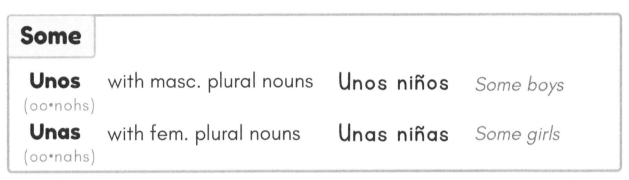

A/An:			
Un (oon)	with masculine nouns	**Un niño** (oon **nee**·nyoh)	*A boy*
Una (oo·nah)	with feminine nouns	**Una niña** (**oo**·nah **nee**·nyah)	*A girl*

Some			
Unos (oo·nohs)	with masc. plural nouns	**Unos niños**	*Some boys*
Unas (oo·nahs)	with fem. plural nouns	**Unas niñas**	*Some girls*

A **Copy and switch the articles:**   The: (el/la) ➡ un/una
The: (los/las) ➡ unos/unas (some)

Las amigas ➡ _____   La cama ➡ _____   El pie ➡ _____

Los libros ➡ _____   El tío ➡ _____   La falda ➡ _____

La puerta ➡ _____   El jardín ➡ _____   La mano ➡ _____

B **Circle the correct article.**

- **una** ○ **un**   familia *A family*
- **unos** ○ **unas** servilletas *Some napkins*
- **un** ○ **una** plato *A plate*

- **una** ○ **un**   cabeza *A head*
- **unos** ○ **unas** calcetines *Some socks*
- **un** ○ **una** abrigo *A coat*

C **Circle the correct article.**

1. Tengo **unos/unas** zapatos negros.

2. ¿Tienes **un/una** lápiz?

3. Mi familia tiene **un/una** casa muy grande. (very big)

4. Tenemos **unos/unas** amigas *muy amables.* (very kind)

Let's practice some more!

A **Translate using un, una, unos, unas:**

1. A sister : _____
2. A mother : _____
3. Some students: _____
4. A computer : _____
5. Some stairs: _____
6. A kitchen: _____
7. An arm : _____

8. A nose: _____
9. A backyard: _____
10. A bathroom: _____
11. A hand: _____
12. Some houses: _____
13. A head: _____
14. A leg: _____

(!) For an unquantifiable amount of something use:
"un poco de" (a little of) instead of *unos/unas*
(oon **poh**·koh deh)

B **Translate using "un poco de":** (ex: **some** milk = **un poco de** leche)

1. Some bread: _____
2. Some meat: _____
3. Some chicken: _____

4. Rice: _____
5. Some water: _____
6. Some fish: _____

C **Complete with the correct article (un/una/unos/unas).**

1. Tengo _____ casa.
2. Tienes _____ teléfono negro.
3. Ella tiene _____ lápiz azul.
4. Tenemos _____ sillón verde.
5. ¿Ud. tiene _____ hermana?

6. Tienen _____ casa grande.
7. Ellas tienen _____ telévision.
8. Tenemos _____ jardín grande.
9. Tenemos _____ libros.
10. Tengo _____ cuadernos rojos.

SENTENCE BUILDER

Time for more practice. Here's are a few new words:

- There is/are: **Hay** (ay)
- now : **ahora** (ah•oh•rah)
- To eat: **Comer** (koh•mehr)
- Something: **Algo** (ahl•goh)

- I want: **Quiero** (kyeh•roh)
- You want (inf.): **Quieres** (kyeh•rehs)
- You (form.)/He/She wants: **Quiere** (kyeh•reh)
- In/On : **en** (ehn)

1. In the kitchen, there is some food in the refrigerator.

2. There are five cups and some plates on the table.

3. The food is on the table. <u>Come</u>, it's time to eat. (talking to a group)

4. In my plate, there is meat and rice. I want to eat.

5. The forks and the spoons are on the table.

6. There is milk in the saucepan.

7. I want to eat something now.

8. There are glasses and water on the table.

9. I want to eat some fish and some bread now.

10. There is chicken and rice in the fridge.

ASKING QUESTIONS

In spanish, the simplest way to ask a question is to raise your intonation toward the end of your sentence. In writing, you must put question marks around your question, the one at the beginning is upside down.

Quieres comer.	*You want to eat.*
¿ Quieres comer **?**	*You want to eat.*

Do you remember the phrase ¿**Cómo** estás? *(How are you?)* "Cómo" means **how**.

A　　**Translate these sentences using "Cómo":**

1. – How is Miguel?　_____

　　– He's doing well?　_____

2. – How is the food?　_____

　　– It's delicious.　_____
　　(deliciosa)

3. How is the chicken?:　_____

　　– It's perfect.　_____
　　(perfecto)

> **ESTAR**
> 1. Location *(People & things)*
> 2. Health
> 3. Opinion
> 4. Mood/condition...

Don't forget the 2 question marks!

Other helpful question words:

• Why: **Por qué** (por keh)	¿Por qué estás aquí?	*Why are you here?*
• What: **Qué** (keh)	¿Qué es esto?	*What is this?*
• Were: **Dónde** (don·deh)	¿Dondé esta mi teléfono?	*Where is my phone?*

B **Fill in the blanks with the correct question word:**

- ¿ _____ quieres?　*What do you want?*

- ¿ _____ está tu hermana?　*Where is your sister?*

- ¿ _____ quieren comer esto?　*Why do you (all) want to eat this?*

- ¿ _____ está su casa?　*Where is his house?*

- ¿ _____ no quieres comer?　*Why don't you want to eat?*

> Exclamative sentences also are also sandwiched between 2 exclamation points, with the first one being upside down:
> ¡Qué bonita! *¡How cute!*

Las frutas (lahs **froo**•tahs) — Fruits

>> **Read outloud then write twice.**

La manzana
(mahn•**sah**•nah)

_____

_____

El plátano
(**plah**•tah•noh)

Also: la banana

_____

_____

La naranja
(nah•**rahn**•Hah)

_____

_____

La fresa
(freh•sah)

_____

_____

Las uvas
(**oo**•bahs)

_____

_____

La pera
(**peh**•rah)

_____

_____

La sandía
(sahn•**dee**•ah)

_____

_____

El limón
(lee•**mon**)

_____

_____

El durazno
(doo.rahs.no)

Also: El melocotón

_____

_____

Las frutas _____   *Fruits*   _____

Connect the words.

The peach •	El plátano
The banana •	La sandía
The apple •	La fresa
The strawberry •	La pera
The watermelon •	El limón
The grapes •	Las uvas
The lemon •	El durazno
The orange •	La manzana
The pear •	La naranja

Circle the correct article.

- Un o Una durazno
- Un o Una manzana
- Un o Una pera
- Un o Una naranja

- Un o Una plátano
- Un o Una sandía
- Un o Una fresa
- Un o Una limón
- Uno o Unas uvas

Translate.

The lemon	The apple	The watermelon
The strawberry	The pear	The banana
The grapes	The orange	The peach

Las verduras (behr•**doo**•rahs) — Vegetables

>> <u>**Read outloud then write twice.**</u>

La papa
(**pah**•pah)

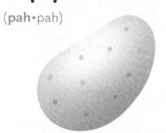

Spain: "patata"

_____

_____

El tomate
(toh•**mah**•teh)

Mexico: "Jitomate"

_____

_____

El pepino
(peh•**pee**•noh)

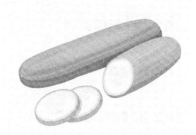

_____

_____

La zanahoria
(sah•nah•**oh**•rya)

_____

_____

La cebolla
(seh•**boh**•yah)

_____

_____

El maíz
(mah•**ees**)

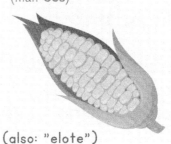

(also: "elote")

_____

_____

La lechuga
(leh•**choo**•gah)

_____

_____

La calabacita
(kah•lah•bah•**see**.tah)

Also:
"calabacín"

_____

_____

Los chícharos
(**chee**•chah•rohs)

Spain: "los guisantes"

_____

_____

Las verduras _____ *Vegetables* _____

*Also:
los vegetales*

65

Connect the words.

The onion •	El maïz
The peas •	La lechuga
The lettuce •	La zanahoria
The corn •	Los chícharos
The green beans •	La papa
The cucumber •	El pepino
The tomato •	La cebolla
The carrot •	La calabacita
The potato •	El tomate

Circle the correct article.

• Un   o Una   cebolla

• Un   o Una   tomate

• Un   o Una   zanahoria

• Un   o Una   pepino

• Un   o Una   papa

• Unos   o Unas   chícharos (guisantes)

• Un   o Una   lechuga

• Un   o Una   maíz

• Un   o Una   calabacita

Translate. (try from memory only!)

The corn

_____

The carrot

_____

The cucumber

_____

The potato

_____

The lettuce

_____

The zucchini

_____

The tomato

_____

The peas

_____

The onion

_____

The vegetables

_____

Otra comida (oh·trah koh·mee·dah) –Other foods

>> **Read outloud then write twice.**

El pastel
(pahs·tehl)

_____

_____

La ensalada
(ehn·sah·lah·dah)

_____

_____

Las papas fritas
(**pah**·pahs free·tahs)

(Spain: patatas fritas)

_____

_____

El queso
(**keh**·soh)

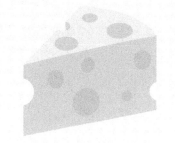

_____

_____

La galleta
(gah·**yeh**·tahs)

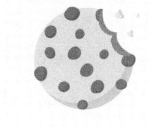

_____

_____

El jugo de naranja
(**Hoo**·goh deh nah·**rahn**·Hah)

_____

_____

El helado
(eh·**lah**·doh)

_____

_____

Leche con chocolate

(leh·cheh
con
choh·koh·**lah**·teh)

_____

_____

El té
(teh)

_____

_____

Connect the words.

The tea •   Leche con chocolate

The ice cream •   Las papas fritas

The cheese •   El pastel

The chocolate milk •   La galleta

The fries •   El queso

The orange juice •   El té

The cake •   El jugo de naranja

The salad •   El helado

The cookie •   La ensalada

Translate adding "some" (a little of): *ex: some water = un poco de agua*

• tea   » _ _ _ _ _ _ _ _ _ _ _ _ _ _

• cheese   » _ _ _ _ _ _ _ _ _ _ _ _ _ _

• ensalada   » _ _ _ _ _ _ _ _ _ _ _ _ _ _

• chocolate » _ _ _ _ _ _ _ _ _ _ _ _ _ _
  milk

• ice cream   » _ _ _ _ _ _ _ _ _ _ _ _ _ _

• french fries » _ _ _ _ _ _ _ _ _ _ _ _ _ _

• orange juice » _ _ _ _ _ _ _ _ _ _ _ _ _ _

• cake   » _ _ _ _ _ _ _ _ _ _ _ _ _ _

• cookies*   » _ _ _ _ _ _ _ _ _ _ _ _ _ _

*(use **unas** with cookies)*

Other foods similar to English: • *los* cereales, la pizza, el sándwich, la sopa, el yogur.
(seh•reh•**ah**•lehs)   (soup)   (yogurt)

Translate.

The tea   The ice cream   The cake

_____   _____   _____

The cheese   The salad   The cookie

_____   _____   _____

The fries   The orange juice   Chocolate milk

_____   _____   _____

SENTENCE BUILDER

Time to practice but first, let's learn the following:

• Please : **Por favor** (pohr·fah·**bohr**)
• Do you want...?: **¿Quieres...?**

• Yes/No: **Sí / No** (see/noh)
• Do you want (form): **¿ (ud.) Quiere...?**

• For: **para** (**pah**·rah)
• We want : **queremos** (keh·**reh**·mohs)

• Thank you: **gracias** (**grahs**·yahs)
• You (pl.)/They want: **quieren** (**kyeh**·rehn)

1. I want some ice cream with strawberries and a banana please.

_____

2. They want water and some food now.

_____

3. Do you want something? – Yes, I want a green apple, please. (you: inf.)

_____

4. For (the) lunch, they want bread with cheese and a salad.

_____

5. Do you want some orange juice for (the) breakfast? – No, thank you.

_____

6. Now we want some cookies and chocolate milk, please.

_____

7. For (the) dinner, I want some meat and peas, please.

_____

8. I want some chicken and rice please.

_____

9. Do you want some tea? – Yes, please. Thank you. (you: form.)

_____

10. Does he want fish and vegetables for (the) dinner?

_____

>> **Read outloud then write twice.**

La primavera
(pree·mah·**beh**·rah)

_____

_____

El verano
(beh·**rah**·noh)

_____

_____

El otoño
(oh·**toh**·nyoh)

_____

_____

El invierno (masc.)
(een·**byehr**·noh)

_____

_____

El sol
(sohl)

_____

_____

La lluvia
(**yoo**·byah)

_____

_____

La nieve
(**nyeh**·beh)

_____

_____

Hace frío
(**ah**·seh **free**·oh)

_____

_____

Hace calor
(**ah**·seh kah·**lohr**)

_____

_____

El tiempo: _____   *The weather (or time)*   _____

Connect the words.

Spring •	El verano
Summer •	La nieve
Fall/Autumn •	La lluvia
Winter •	Hace frío
The sun •	La primavera
The rain •	Hace calor
The snow •	El otoño
It's cold •	El invierno
It's hot •	El sol

⚠ Hace calor/frío: ➡ for weather only.

⚠ To say something is hot/cold: Está caliente/frío)
To say: I'm hot/cold: Tengo calor/frío)

Read carefully and copy.

- In summer: En verano _____ _____
- In fall: En otoño _____ _____
- In winter: En invierno _____ _____
- In spring: En primavera _____ _____

Translate.

The rain

_____

Winter

_____

The sun

_____

Spring

_____

Fall

_____

It's hot

_____

The snow

_____

It's cold

_____

Summer

_____

The weather

_____

>> **Read outloud then write twice.**

El edificio
(eh•dee•**fee**•syoh)

_____

_____

La tienda
(**tyehn**•dah)

_____

_____

El hotel
(oh•**tehl**)

_____

_____

El museo
(moo•**seh**•oh)

_____

_____

El supermercado
(soo•pehr•mehr•**kah**•doh)

_____

_____

El hospital
(ohs•pee•**tahl**

_____

_____

El cine
(**see**•neh)

_____

_____

El restaurante
(rrehs•taw•**rahn**•teh)

_____

_____

La calle
(**kah**•yeh)

_____

_____

La ciudad: _____   *The city*   _____

Connect the words.

The building •	La calle
The store •	El supermercado
The hotel •	El cine
The museum •	La tienda
The supermarket •	El restaurante
The hospital •	El museo
The movie theater •	El edificio
The restaurant •	El hôtel
The street •	El hospital

Circle the correct article.

- El   o   La   hotel
- El   o   La   edificio
- El   o   La   cine
- El   o   La   restaurante

- El   o   La   museo
- El   o   La   tienda
- El   o   La   calle
- El   o   La   hospital
- El   o   La   supermercado

Translate. (from memory)

The hospital	The street	The restaurant
The movie theater	The hotel	The supermarket
The store	The building	The museum

El trabajo (trah·**bah**·Hoh)   – Work

≫ **Read outloud then write twice.**

El doctor
(dok·**tohr**)

_____

_____

La enfermera
(ehn·fehr·**meh**·rah)

_____

_____

El ingeniero
(een·Heh·nyeh·roh)

_____

_____

El bombero
(bohm·**beh**·roh)

_____

_____

El policía
(poh·lee·**see**·yah)

_____

_____

El dentista
(dehn·**tees**·tah)

_____

_____

El gerente   (manager)
(Heh·**rehn**·teh)

_____

_____

La secretaria
(seh·kreh·**tah**·ryah)

_____

_____

El abogado
(ah·boh·**gah**·doh)

_____

_____

El trabajo _____   _Work/Job_   _____

≫ Connect the words.

The doctor •	El ingeniero
The nurse •	El bombero
The engineer •	El gerente
The fireman •	La enfermera
The police officer •	El abogado
The dentist •	La secretaria
The manager •	El policía
The secretary •	El doctor
The lawyer •	El dentista

≫ Read and copy once the opposite gender version.

• Una ingeniera (f.)

• Una gerente (f.)

• Una mujer policía (f.)

(moo.Her poh•lee•**see**•yah)

• Una abogada (f.)

• Una dentista (f.)

• Una doctora (f.)

• Una bombera (f.)

• Un enfermero (m.)

• Un secretario (m.)

≫ Translate.

The dentist (fem.)

_____

The secretary (masc.)

_____

The police man (masc.)

_____

The nurse (fem.)

_____

The manager (masc.)

_____

The doctor (fem.)

_____

The engineer (fem.)

_____

The fireman (masc.)

_____

The lawyer (fem.)

_____

SENTENCE BUILDER (Me gusta/No me gusta)

The simplest way to make a sentence negative is to add "**no**" before the verb:

ex: I'm cold = Tengo frío ➡ I'm not cold = **No** tengo frío

ex: I'm hot = Tengo calor ➡ I'm not hot = **No** tengo calor   (kah·lohr)

- I like: **Me gusta** (meh **goos**·tah)
- I don't like: **No me gusta**
- You like (inf.): **te gusta** (teh **goos**·tah)
  ("you like" formal: **Le** gusta)
- Because: **porque** (pohr·keh)

- I love (something): **Me encanta** (stronger than "like")
- The weather is nice: **Hace** buen tiempo
- It's hot/cold (weather): **Hace calor/ frío**
- Sometimes: **A veces** (ah **beh**·sehs)

1. The weather is nice today. Do you like (the) spring?   (inf.)

2. I love (the) summer because it's hot and I like the sun!

3. The weather is nice in spring but sometimes there is a bit of rain.*

4. It's hot in summer but I like (the) summer.

5. I like (the) winter because I love the snow.

6. I'm cold today but I love the snow. Do you like winter?   (for.)

7. I don't like (the) summer because it's hot. I love (the) fall.

8. I don't like (the) fall and I don't like (the) winter.

9. In fall, it's a little cold but I like the rain.   (a little: un poco)

10. The weather is nice today. I'm hot but I love (the) summer!

*a little bit of/ a bit of: un poco de

- To ask "What do you do for a living? you can say:

   1. ¿A qué te dedicas? ⟹ To answer, remove "a". Ex: *I am a dentist* = Soy dentista.
   (ah keh teh deh•**dee**.kass)

Vocabulary:
- I'm going (to): **(Yo) Voy (a)** (boy ah)
- You're going (to): **(Tú) vas (a)** (bahs ah)
- I'm not going: **No voy**

- Are you going (to)..?= ¿**Vas (a)**..?(inf.)
- to the (+ masc.)... = **al (a + el)**
- The park = **El parque** (pahr•keh)
- at home = **a casa**

1. Are you going home? – I'm going to the park. I'm not going home.

2. <u>Your</u> father is a manager and your mom is a dentist.   (inf.)

3. My aunt is a nurse and my uncle is an engineer.

4. The woman is a lawyer and the man is a fireman.

5. My sister is a secretary and my brother is a policeman.

6. I'm not going to be a teacher, I'm going to be a lawyer. (masc.)

7. There are doctors and nurses in the hospital. (mix.)

8. His father and his children are in the park today.

9. I am at school today but my sister is at home. She's sick.   (think: "in the" school)

10. I want to be a nurse or a doctor. (female)

Los animales (ah•nee•**mah**•lehs)   – Animals

>> **Read outloud then write twice.**

El perro
(**peh**•rroh)

_____

El gato
(**gah**•toh)

_____

El pájaro   (masc.)
(**pah**•Hah•roh)

_____

El conejo
(koh•**neh**•Hoh)

_____

El caballo
(kah•**bah**•yoh)

_____

La vaca
(**bah**•kah)

_____

El cerdo
(**sehr**•doh)

_____
_____

La oveja
(oh•**beh**•Hah)

_____
_____

El ratón
(rah•**tohn**)

_____
_____

El animal _____
The animal   (ah•nee•**mahl**)

Los animales _____
The animals   (ah•nee•**mahl**•lehs)

78

Connect the words.

The dog •	El ratón
The cat •	La oveja
The bird •	El gato
The bunny •	El pájaro
The horse •	El cerdo
The cow •	La vaca
The pig •	El conejo
The sheep •	El caballo
The mouse •	El perro

Translate using *un* or *una*.

- a dog _____
- a cat _____
- a bird _____
- a rabbit _____

- A horse _____
- A cow _____
- A pig _____
- A sheep _____
- A mouse _____

Translate.

	An animal	(The) Animals
The bunny	A cat	A pig
A horse	The sheep	The mouse
The cow	A bird	A dog

Los animales salvajes — Wild Animals
(ah•nee•**mah**•lehs sahl•**bah**•Hehs)

>> <u>**Read outloud then write twice.**</u>

Un tigre
(**tee**•greh)

_____

_____

Un león
(leh•**ohn**)

_____

_____

Un elefante
(eh•leh•**fahn**•teh)

_____

_____

Una jirafa
(hee•**rah**•fah)

_____

_____

El cocodrilo
(koh•koh•**dree**•loh)

_____

_____

Un oso
(**oh**•soh)

_____

_____

Un delfín
(dehl•**feen**)

_____

_____

Un tiburón
(tee•boo•**rohn**)

_____

_____

Una ballena
(bah•**yeh**•nah)

_____

_____

El animal salvaje _____
The wild animal   (ah•nee•**mahl**)

Los animales salvajes _____
The wild animals   (ah•nee•**mahl**•lehs sahl•**bah**•Hehs)

≫ Connect the words.

The tiger •	El cocodrilo
The lion •	El tigre
The elephant •	La ballena
The giraffe •	El oso
The crocodile •	El tiburón
The bear •	El león
The dolphin •	La jirafa
The shark •	El elefante
The whale •	El delfín

≫ Translate with *un* or *una*:

- A tigre: _____

- A lion: _____

- An elephant: _____

- A giraffe: _____

- A crocodile: _____

- A bear: _____

- A dolphin: _____

- A shark: _____

- A whale: _____

≫ Translate. (Use your memory!)

The shark

_____

A whale

_____

A giraffe

_____

The lion

_____

A tiger

_____

The bear

_____

Wild animals

_____

The crocodile

_____

A dolphin

_____

The elephant

_____

>> **Read outloud then write twice.**

El árbol
(**ahr**·bohl)

_____

_____

La flor
(flohr)

_____

_____

El césped   (fem.)
(**sehs**·pehd)

_____

_____

La montaña
(mohn·**tah**·nyah)

_____

_____

El bosque
(**bohs**·keh)

_____

_____

El mar
(mahr)

_____

_____

La playa
(**plah**·yah)

_____

_____

El cielo
(**syeh**·loh)

_____

_____

El insecto
(een·**sehk**·toh)

_____

_____

La naturaleza _____   *Nature* _____

Connect the words.

The tree •   El mar

The flower •   El cielo

The grass/lawn •   El bosque

The mountain •   El árbol

The forest •   El césped

The sea •   La playa

The beach •   La montaña

The sky •   La flor

The insect •   El insecto

Translate with *un* or *una*:

- A tree: _____
- A flower: _____
- A lawn: _____
- A mountain: _____

- A forest: _____
- A sea: _____
- A beach: _____
- A sky: _____
- An insect: _____

Translate.

The sea
_____

A flower
_____

A tree
_____

A mountain
_____

The forest
_____

The insect
_____

The grass
_____

A beach
_____

The sky
_____

Nature _____

El transporte (trahns·**porh**·teh)   –Transportation

El carro
(**kah**·rroh)

Also: El coche / El auto
(**koh**·cheh/**ow**·toh)

_____

_____

El camión
(kah·**myohn**)

_____

_____

La motocicleta
(moh·toh·see·**kleh**·tah)

Also: La moto

_____

_____

El tren
(trehn)

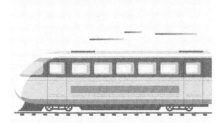

_____

_____

El avión   (masc.)
(ah·**byohn**)

_____

_____

La bicicleta
(bee·see·**kleh**·tah)

_____

_____

El barco
(**bahr**·koh)

_____

_____

El autobús
(ow·toh·**boos**)

_____

_____

El metro
(**meh**·troh)

_____

_____

≫ Connect the words.

The bus •	La motocicleta
The boat •	El tren
The car •	El camión
The motorcycle •	El metro
The train •	El avión
The truck •	El barco
The subway •	El autobús
The bicycle •	La bicicleta
The plane •	El carro

≫ Translate with *un* or *una*:

- A car: _____

- A truck: _____

- A plane : _____

- A train: _____

- A motorcycle: _____

- A bicycle: _____

- A boat: _____

- A bus: _____

- A subway: _____

≫ Translate. (adjectives after nouns here)

A yellow bus	The subway	The green bicycle
A big boat	The red car	The train
The black motorcycle	The big plane	A black truck

SENTENCE BUILDER

Let's write more sentences. You will use this useful vocabulary:

- The fish: **El Pez /Los peces (pl.)**
- (Do)You like...?: **¿Te gusta...?** (inf.)
- I/You like + plural: **Me/Te gusta̲n ...**
- a lot: **mucho** (moo·choh)
- a lot of + masc./plural: **mucho/muchos**
- a lot of + fem./plural: **mucha/muchas**

<u>Plurals:</u>
- Add an S to nouns/adjectives ending in a vowel: La montaña: Las montañas
- Add an -ES to nouns/adjectives ending in a consonant: El animal: Los animales
- Wors ending in -N lose their accent in the plural: El avión: Los aviones

1. You have a lot of animals in your house! (inf.)

2. Do you like*animals? -Yes, I like animals a lot. (place **a lot** after **like**)

3. There is a white car in the garage.

4. I love*animals but I don't like sharks! (see above for plural)

5. In the sea, there are sharks, whales, dolphins and fishes*. (fishes: peces)

6. In my city, there are buildings, a hospital and a supermarket.

7. In my street, there are a lot of restaurants and a movie theater.

8. I like*horses and cows but I don't like pigs.

9. There are a lot of birds in the sky today.

10. In my street, there are a lot of cars, motorcycles and trucks.

* Must add "**the**" after **like / love** + **noun** (ex: Me gustan **los** animales/ me gusta **el** helado)

Los verbos (behr·bohs) — Verbs

>> **Read outloud then write twice.**

IR   To go
(eer)

_____

_____

"Ir <u>a</u>" if followed by location or verb.

COMER
(koh·**mehr**)

_____

_____

DORMIR
(dohr·**meer**)

_____

_____

TOMAR
(toh·**mahr**)

Also/Spain:
Beber
(beh·**behr**)

_____

_____

"Tomar" also means to take/grab

JUGAR
(Hoo·**gahr**)

_____

_____

VER   Watch/see
(behr)

_____

_____

HACER   To do
(ah·**sehr**)

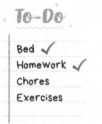

To-Do

Bed ✓
Homework ✓
Chores
Exercises

_____

_____

LEER
(leh·**ehr**)

_____

_____

ESCRIBIR
(ehs·kree·**beer**)

Once upon a time...

_____

_____

To go •	Dormir
To eat •	Leer
To sleep •	Hacer
To drink •	Ir
To play •	Jugar
To watch/See •	Tomar/ Beber
To do/ To make •	Escribir
To read •	Comer
To write •	Ver

"I would like" + verb = **Me gustaría + verb** (meh goos•tah•ree•ah)

>> **Translate the phrases.**

I want to read	I would like to do...	Do you want to play? (inf.)
I want to sleep	I would like to go...	Do you want to drink something? (inf.)
I want to watch	I would like to write...	Do you want to eat? (form.)

>> **Translate.**

To read	To sleep	To play
To drink	To write	To go
To eat	To watch	To do/To make

88

Actividades (ahk·tee·bee·**dah**·dehs) — Activities

>> **Read outloud then write twice.**

Hacer ejercicio
(soh·**fah**)

_____

_____

Bailar
(bay·**lahr**)

_____

_____

Jugar tenis
(Hoo·**gahr** teh·nees)

_____

_____

Correr
(koh·**rrehr**)

_____

_____

Comprar
(kohm·**prahr**)

_____

_____

Viajar
(byah·**Hahr**)

_____

_____

Hablar
(ah·**blahr**)

_____

_____

Andar en bicicleta
(ahn·**dahr** ehn bee·see·**kleh**·tah)

_____

_____

Nadar
(nah·**dahr**)

_____

_____

Connect the words.

To swim •	Comprar
To play tennis •	Correr
To buy •	Hablar
To speak/talk •	Hacer ejercicio
To run •	Jugar tenis
To ride a bike •	Viajar
To exercise •	Nadar
To travel •	Bailar
To dance •	Ir en bicicleta

Translate the phrases.

I'm going to play tennis	I would like to buy a house.	(Do) you want to talk? (inf.)
I'm going to exercise	I would like to ride a bike.	(Do) you want to swim? (inf.)
I want to run	I would like to travel.	(Do) you want to dance? (form.)

Also: Hacer yoga/ jugar golf/ jugar básketball/ jugar fútball (soccer)...

Translate.

To travel	To buy	To dance
To ride a bike	To exercise	To talk
To run	To play tennis	To swim

Adjetivos (ahd·Heh·**tee**·bohs)   -Adjectives

>> **Read outloud then write twice.** (with masculine / feminine)

Grande (big)
(**grahn**·deh)

_____

_____

Pequeño/Pequeña
(peh·**keh**·nyoh/ah)

_____

_____

simpática
(seem·**pah**·tee·kah)

_____

_____

Rápido/Rápida
(rrah·pee·doh/ah)

_____

_____

Bueno/Buena
(**bweh**·noh/**bweh**·nah)

Buen before a masc./sing noun

_____

_____

Feliz
(feh·lees)

_____

_____

Hermoso/Hermosa
(ehr·**moh**·soh/ehr·**moh**·sah)

_____

_____

Fácil
(**fah**·seel)

_____

_____

Difícil
(dee·**fee**·seel)

_____

_____

*ome adjectives do not change in the feminine form but do take an -**s** or -**es** in the plural.*

>> Connect the words.

Big/Large •   Difícil

Small •   Hermoso/a

Nice/friendly •   Simpático/a

Fast •   Grande

Good •   Fácil

Difficult / Hard •   Buen/Bueno/a

Handsome/ •
Beautiful   Feliz

Easy •   Pequeño/a

Happy •   Rápido/a

>> Translate: Place adjectives after the nouns (except "good").

• A friendly cousin: _____
(masc.)

• A beautiful woman: _____

• A big house: _____

• Little girls: _____

• A good teacher: _____
(fem.)   place "good" before the noun

• A fast car: _____

• A happy child: _____

• A difficult exam:* _____

• An easy exam:* _____

*exam: examen (ehk•sah•mehn)

It's very...: **Es muy** ...
It's not very ...: **No es muy** ...

>> Translate.

It's very fast (masc.)	Big/Large	It's very good (masc.)
_____	_____	_____
It's very difficult	Happy	It's not very easy
_____	_____	_____
Nice/Friendly (fem.)	It's very small (masc.)	A handsome man
_____	_____	_____

SENTENCE BUILDER

Let's write more sentences with these helpful new words:

- With me: **Conmigo** (kohn•**mee**•goh)
- With me: **Contigo** (kohn•**tee**•goh)

- Me: **Yo** (yoh)
- too/also: **También** (tahm•**byehn**)

I like: • Me gust**a** + **sing**. noun(or verb)
     • Me gusta**n** + **plu**. noun

I love: • Me encant**a** + **sing**. noun(or verb)
     • Me encanta**n** + **plu**. noun

>> **Translate**.

1. My brother also wants to go to the movies with you.

_____

2. Do you want to eat some ice cream now? – Me too! (inf.)

_____

3. I want to go home. I want to read my book in my bedroom. ("Ir a")

_____

4. He wants to do his homework on his desk.

_____

5. I love to dance. Do you want to dance with me now? (inf.)

_____

6. I'm very happy! Today my homework is very easy!

_____

7. Come here please. I want to speak with you now. (to one person)

_____

8. Do you like to drink milk <u>for</u> breakfast? (inf.) (translate as: "in the" breakfast)

_____

9. I love motorcycles. I have one in my house.

_____

10. I love to exercise and to swim. Sometimes, I also* like to run.

_____

*(place "also" before "I like")

Great Job! This is your last Sentence Builder! This one is a bit longer and will challenge your memory! We will use vocabulary you learned *throughout* this book. If you can't remember some words, just take a look at the vocabulary list that follows this quiz. **You can do it!** (Answers p.113 - 115)

1. In the forest, there are bears, birds and bunnies.

2. We have a black dog and a white cat in our house.

3. In my bedroom, there is a big bed, a black desk and a computer.

4. I am a <u>good</u> student. I have my books, my pen and a notebook.* (masc.)

5. In <u>your</u> house, there is a large backyard and a garage. (form.)

6. They have a very large tv in the living room.

7. Hi! How are <u>you</u>? My name is Sam, and <u>you</u>? (inf.)

8. Today is Wednesday. I have a difficult exam at school! (in the school)

9. I am sick today. I don't have fever but I have a stomachache.

10. My building is very big but my house is very small.

11. I want to go to (in) my bedroom now. I want to sleep in my bed.

*bueno is "buen" before a masc. sing. noun

12. My father is very big, he is a fireman.

13. My uncle is a dentist and my aunt is a teacher.

14. My sister is ten years old. She is beautiful and very nice.

15. There is chicken, rice and peas in his plate. (Do)You want to eat too?
(inf.)

16. I want an apple and I want to drink some milk please.

17. There is a little insect in the kitchen!

18. I would like to travel with some friends in summer .

19. I love to drink chocolate milk in winter.

20. Your children are very beautiful! What are their names? (form.)

21. The chicken is very good! I would like to eat a bit more please*.

22. For (the) breakfast, I want some orange juice and bread with eggs.

23. For (the) dinner, I want pasta, some cheese and a salad please.

24. For (the) lunch) there are potatoes, zucchini and meat.

*a bit more: un poco más

25. Your car is very big but it's not very fast. (for.)

26. Your grandfather and my grandmather are at her house. (inf.)

27. Why are there a lot of birds in the sky today? (think: why there is...)

28. In summer, I am very happy because the weather is nice.

29. I don't like the weather today because there is a lot of snow!

30. It's very easy! Come with me! (to a group)

31. There are a lot of people in the subway today. I dont like (it). (omit "it")

32. Where are my black socks and my red shoes?

33. I love nature but I don't like insects!

34. My homework is very difficult! And I have a lot of homework today!

35. Do <u>you</u> want to go to the movies with me today? (pl.)

36. Why do <u>you</u> want to go to the supermarket? - Because I want to buy cookies. (inf.)

37. Sometimes I like to watch (the) tv in my bedroom with my sister.

38. My <u>cousin</u> has a green car and a yellow motorcycle. (masc.)

39. I want to buy socks, pants and underwear at (in) the store.

40. I like (the) trains and (the) planes because I love to travel.

41. In winter, I like to play in the snow with my family.

42. You're going to the park? Do you want to play soccer with me? (inf.)

43. I would like to buy a lot of books because I love to read.

44. Today I want to make (do) a cake for my mother.

45. I'm going to the beach with my family and some friends.

46. I love the mountains and the sea. (The) Nature is beautiful!

47. I like my school but I don't like to do my homework.

48. I'm hot today! I don't like the weather in summer. I like (the) spring!

49. Sometimes I go to the park because I like to play and ride a bike.

50. I love to speak Spanish! (Spanish = Español) (ehs•pah•**nyohl**)

All done!

Congratulations on completing your Spanish workbook! You went from absolute beginner to learning **over 400 words**!

Pat yourself in the back for completing this very important first step.

You can now say simple sentences with the verb to be, to have, to want and ask for things you "would like". You can introduce yourself, talk about your family, the weather, food, travel and much more!

It takes time and practice to acquire a new language, so you should increase your contact with the Spanish language. <u>Keep learning new words</u>, <u>read books</u>, <u>watch movies</u>, <u>listen to Podcasts</u>, YouTube videos, <u>cartoons and whatever you normally like to do but **in Español!**</u>

Before you know it, this language will become so familiar that it will no longer be "foreign" to you!

Be sure to check out **our other Spanish learning books on Amazon**. Keep an eye out for **Level 2** of this series, where you will learn a ton of verbs, useful conjugation and boost your speaking skills!

I truly want to help you learn because I LOVE languages. I have learned several languages on my own so I know both the struggles and the satisfaction of being able to converse in a language you worked so hard to acquire. Believe in yourself, be consistent and you will reach your language goals!

Thank you for trusting me in your language journey!

Mimi

LANGUAGE LEARNING TIPS from Mimi!

- Practice the new words daily by making **simple sentences** as you did in this book (even just 10 to 20 a a day) and review the Word List periodically so you don't forget them. You can even make **flashcards** for quick review.
- **Watch movies** or cartoons in Spanish with subtitles.
- Try the free chrome extensions such as "Language Reactor". It has a catalogue of videos in YouTube and Netflix (requires Netflix subscription). It allows you to choose 2 subtitles. You can watch a movie in **Spanish with subtitles** both in English and Spanish to read and understand better. It's a great tool, especially for beginners.
- **Listen** to songs, radio or podcasts in Spanish.
- **Read books in Spanish**, starting with simple ones for young readers.
- **Practice with other Spanish speakers, or even by yourself**! The best way to learn to speak Spanish is to actually speak **in Spanish**. Starting with very simple sentences. It's uncomfortable at first but you will be amazed at how your brain will adapt and you will gradually speak better and better.
- **Talk to yourself in Spanish!** I recommend taping yourself having mini "monologues" talking about things that relate to you and your life (even just 3 or 4 minutes videos), then rewatch those videos so you can **review and translate the words you didn't know**. Then repeat the whole monologue with this new vocabulary. This is one of my favorite exercise to help me speak with more confidence and spontaneity in languages I'm studying. I highly recommend this exercise!

There is no quick fix, learning a language is a long process so just enjoy it! Surround yourself with Spanish, be consistent and you will see results!
¡Buena suerte! (Good luck!)

Got a minute?
Please consider **leaving a review on Amazon,**
I'd love to hear how you enjoyed this book!
¡Gracias!

Conjugation - Present tense

• TO WANT: QUERER

- I	– (Yo) Quiero
- You (inf.)	– (Tu) Quieres
- You (form.)	– (Ud.) Quiere
- He/She	– (Él / Ella) Quiere
- We	– (Nosotros) Queremos
- You (pl.)	– (Uds.) Quieren
- They	– (Ellos / Ellas) Quieren

• Vosotros/as **queréis** (Spain)

• TO LIKE: GUSTAR

- I	– Me gusta(n)
- You (inf.)	– Te gusta(n)
- You (form.)	– Le gusta(n)
- He/She	– Le gusta(n)
- We	– Nos gusta(n)
- You (pl.)	– Les gusta(n)
- They	– Les gusta(n)

• add –n when followed by a plural noun
• Vosotros/as: **Les gustáis** (Spain)

• TO GO: IR

- I	– (Yo) Voy
- You (inf.)	– (Tu) Vas
- You (form.)	– (Ud.) Va
- He/She	– (Él / Ella) Va
- We	– (Nosotros) Vamos
- You (pl.)	– (Uds.) Van
- They	– (Ellos / Ellas) Van

• Vosotros/as **queréis** (Spain)

• TO DO / MAKE: HACER

- I	– (Yo) Hago
- You (inf.)	– (Tu) Haces
- You (form.)	– (Ud.) Hace
- He/She	– (Él / Ella) Hace
- We	– (Ns.) Hacemos
- You (pl.)	– (Uds.) Hacen
- They	– (Ellos/Ellas) Hacen

• Vosotros/as **hacéis** (Spain)

• TO SPEAK: HABLAR

- I	– (Yo) Hablo
- You (inf.)	– (Tu) Hablas
- You (form.)	– (Ud.) Habla
- He/She	– (Él / Ella) Habla
- We	– (Nosotros) Hablamos
- You (pl.)	– (Uds.) Hablan
- They	– (Ellos / Ellas) Hablan

• Vosotros/as **habláis** (Spain)

• TO EAT: COMER

- I	– (Yo) Como
- You (inf.)	– (Tu) Comes (koh·mehs)
- You (form.)	– (Ud.) Come
- He/She	– (Él / Ella) Come
- We	– (Ns.) Comemos
- You (pl.)	– (Uds.) Comen
- They	– (Ellos/Ellas) Comen

• Vosotros/as **coméis** (Spain)

0. Cero	10. Diez	20. Veinte	30. Treinta	40. Cuarenta
1. Uno	11. Once	21. Veintiuno	31. Treinta y uno	41. Cuarenta y uno
2. Dos	12. Doce	22. Veintidós	32. Treinta y dos	42. Cuarenta y dos
3. Tres	13. Trece	23. Veintitrés	33. Treinta y tres	43. Cuarenta y tres
4. Cuatro	14. Catorce	24. Veinticuatro	34. Treinta y cuatro	44. Cuarenta y cuatro
5. Cinco	15. Quince	25. Veinticinco	35. Treinta y cinco	45. Cuarenta y cinco
6. Seis	16. Dieciseis	26. Veintiséis	36. Treinta y seis	46. Cuarenta y seis
7. Siete	17. Diecisiete	27. Veintisiete	37. Treinta y siete	47. Cuarenta y siete
8. Ocho	18. Diecisiocho	28. Veintiocho	38. Treinta y ocho	48. Cuarenta y ocho
9. Nueve	19. Diecinueve	29. Veintinueve	39. Treinta y nueve	49. Cuarenta y nueve

50. Cincuenta

51. Cincuenta y uno
52. Cincuenta y dos
53. Cincuenta y tres
54. Cincuenta y cuatro
55. Cincuenta y cinco
56. Cincuenta y seis
57. Cincuenta y siete
58. Cincuenta y ocho
59. Cincuenta y nueve

60. Sesenta

61. Sesenta y uno
62. Sesenta y dos
63. Sesenta y tres
64. Sesenta y cuatro
65. Sesenta y cinco
66. Sesenta y seis
67. Sesenta y siete
68. Sesenta y ocho
69. Sesenta y nueve

70. Setenta

71. Setenta y uno
72. Setenta y dos
73. Setenta y tres
74. Setenta y cuatro
75. Setenta y cinco
76. Setenta y seis
77. Setenta y siete
78. Setenta y ocho
79. Setenta y nueve

80. Ochenta

81. Ochenta y uno
82. Ochenta y dos
83. Ochenta y tres
84. Ochenta y cuatro
85. Ochenta y cinco
86. Ochenta y seis
87. Ochenta y siete
88. Ochenta y ocho
89. Ochenta y nueve

90. Noventa

91. Noventa y uno
92. Noventa y dos
93. Noventa y tres
94. Noventa y cuatro
95. Noventa y cinco
96. Noventa y seis
97. Noventa y siete
98. Noventa y ocho
99. Noventa y nueve

100. Cien

200. Doscientos
300. Trescientos
400. Cuatrocientos
500. Quinientos
600. Seiscientos
700. Setecientos
800. Ochocientos
900. Novecientos
1000. Mil

LA SEMANA

Monday – lunes
Tuesday – martes
Wednesday – miercoles
Thursday – jueves
Friday – viernes
Saturday – sábado
Sunday – domingo

Today – Hoy
The week – La semana
The day – El día
It is – Es

LOS MESES

January – enero
February – febrero
March – marzo
April – abril
May – mayo
June – junio
July – julio
August – agosto
September – septiembre
October – octubre
Novembre – noviembre
December – diciembre

ARTICLES

The (masc.) – El
The (fem.) – La
The (pl./masc) – Los
The (pl./fem.) – Las

A/An (masc.) – Un
A/An (fem.) – Una

Plural/ Some – Unos/Unas
– un poco de

POSSESSIVES (sing/pl.):

My: – mi / mis
Your (inf.): – tu / tus
Your (form.): – su / sus
His /Her: – su / sus
Our: – nuestro/nuestros
– nuestra /nuestras
Your (pl.): – su / sus
Their: –su / sus

PERSONAL PRONOUNS

· I – Yo
· You (form.) – Usted
· You (inf) – Tú
· He –Él
· She – Ella

· We (formal) – Nosotros
· You (pl.) – Ustedes
(vosotros/as in Spain)
· They (masc./mix) – Ellos
· They (fem.) – Ellas

SER

· I am – (Yo) Soy

· You are (inf.) – (Tú) Eres

· He/She/You (form.) are –Él/Ella/Ud. es

· We are – (Ns) Somos

· You (pl.)*/They are – Uds./Ellos/Ellas son

* · **Vosotros/as sois** (Spain)

ESTAR

· I am – (Yo) Estoy

· You are (inf.) – (Tú) Estás

· He/She/You (form.) are –Él/Ella/Ud. está

· We are – (Ns) Estamos

· You (pl.)*/They are – Uds./Ellos/Ellas Están

* · **Vosotros/as estáis** (Spain)

GREETINGS / CONVERSATION

- Hello/Hi! – ¡Hola!
- Good Morning – Buenos días
- Good evening – Buenas tardes
- Goodbye – Adios
- How are you? – ¿Cómo estás?
- How are you? (form.) – ¿Cómo está usted?
- (I'm) doing well, thanks
  – Estoy bien, gracias
- Very good, thank you
  – Muy bien, gracias.
- And you? (inf.) – ¿Y tú?
- And you? (form.) – ¿Y usted?
- Bad – Mal
- Not very good – No tan bien

- See you later – Hasta luego
- See you! – ¡Nos vemos!
- What's your name? (inf.)
  – ¿Cómo te llamas?
- What's your name? (form.)
  – ¿Cómo se llama usted?
- My name is… – Me llamo…
- How old are you? (form.)
  – ¿Cuántos años tiene?
- How old are you? (inf.)
  – ¿Cuántos años tienes?
- I'm … years old – Tengo … años
- Madam/Mrs – Señora
- Mister/Sir –Señor

TENER (have)

- I have – (Yo) Tengo
- You have (form.) – (Ud.) tiene
- You have (inf.) – (Tú) tienes
- He/She – (Él/Ella) tiene

- We have – (Ns.) Tenemos
- You have (pl.) – (Uds.) Tienen
- They have – (Ellos / Ellas) Tienen

- **Vosotros/as tenéis** (Spain)

SENTENCE STARTERS / CONNECTORS

- I would like – Me gustaría
- Do you want…? – ¿Quieres …?
- I/You want – Quiero/Quieres
- I like – Me gusta(n)
- I love – Me encanta(n)
- I don't like – No me gusta

- There is/are – Hay
- Please – Por favor
- Because – Porque
- Yes / No – Si / No
- Sometimes – A veces
- Now – Ahora

- Very –Muy
- But – Pero
- On – En
- Or – O
- For – para
- A lot – Mucho

LA FAMILIA / FAMILY

The mother – La madre
The father – El padre
The brother – El hermano
The sister – La hermana
The uncle – El tío
The aunt – La tía
The grandfather – El abuelo
The grandmother – La abuela
The family – La familia

LA CASA / HOUSE

The house – La casa
The kitchen – La cocina
The living room – La sala
The bedroom – La habitación
The bathroom – El baño
The restrooms – El inodoro
The backyard – El jardín
The garage – La cochera
The stairs – Las escaleras

EN LA CASA / IN THE HOUSE

The couch – El sillón
The table – La mesa
The chair – La silla
The window – La ventana
The door – La puerta
The bed – La cama
The phone – Le teléfono
The tv – La televisión / La tele
The computer – La computadora

LA ESCUELA / SCHOOL

The classroom – El salón de clase
The teacher – El / La profesor/a
The desk – El escritorio
The homework – La tarea
The book – El libro
The notebook – El cuaderno
The pen – La lapicera
The pencil – El lápiz (SP: boli)
The student – El / La estudiante

EL CUERPO / THE BODY

The head – La cabeza
The eyes – Los ojos
The nose – La nariz
The mouth – La boca
The stomach – El estómago
The arm – El brazo
The hand – La mano
The leg – La pierna
The foot – El pie

LOS COLORES / COLORS

Blue – azul
White – blanco
Red – Rojo
Black – Negro
Green – Verde
Yellow – Amarillo
Orange – Anaranjado/Naranja
Brown – Marrón / café
Pink – Rosado / Rosa

LA ROPA / CLOTHES

The coat - El abrigo

The pants - Los pantalones

The t-shirt - La camiseta   Sweater

The dress - El vestido   - El suéter

The skirt - La falda   Jacket

The pjs - El pijama   -La chaqueta

The underwear - La ropa interior

The socks - Los calcetines

The shoes - Los zapatos

EN LA MESA / ON THE TABLE

The plate - El plato

The fork - El tenedor

The knife - El cuchillo

The spoon - La cuchara

The glass/cup - El vaso

The napkin - La servilleta

The food - La comida

The saucepan - La cacerola

The bottle - La botella

LAS FRUTAS

The apple - La manzana

The banana - El plátano / La banana

The orange - La naranja

The strawberry - La fresa

The grapes - Las uvas

The pear - La pera

The watermelon - La sandía

The lemon - El limón

The peach - El durazno (melocotón)

LA GENTE / LA COMIDA PEOPLE MEALS

The man - El hombre   People -

The woman - La mujer   La gente

The kids - Los niños   Amigo/a

The boy - El niño   - friend

The girl - La niña   Primo/a

The baby - El bebé   -cousin

The breakfast - El desayuno

The lunch - El almuerzo   person -

The dinner - La cena   persona

LA COMIDA / FOOD

The bread - El pan

The eggs - Los huevos

The meat - La carne

The chicken - El pollo

The fish - El pescado

The rice - El arroz

The pasta - La pasta

The milk - La leche

The water - El agua

LAS VERDURAS

The potato - La papa / patata

The tomato - La tomate /Jitomate

The cucumber - El pepino

The carrot - La zanahoria

The onion - La cebolla

The corn - El maïz

The lettuce - La lechuga

The peas - Los chícharos / guisantes

The zucchini - La calabacita (calabacín)

OTRA COMIDA

The cake - El plato

Salad - La ensalada

Fries - Las papas fritas

The cheese - El queso

The cookie - La galleta

The ice cream - El helado

The orange juice - El jugo de naranja

Chocolate milk - Leche con chocolate

The tea - El té

Extra:

Los cereales

La pizza

La sopa

El yogur

EL TIEMPO / THE WEATHER

Spring - La primavera

Summer - El verano

Fall - El otoño

Winter - El invierno

The sun - El sol

The rain - La lluvia

The snow - La nieve

It's hot - Hace calor

It's cold - Hace frío

LA CIUDAD / THE CITY

The building - El edificio

The store - La tienda

The hotel - El hotel

The school - La escuela

The supermarket - El supermercado

The hospital - El hospital

The movie theater - El cine

The restaurant - El restaurante

The street - La calle

LOS TRABAJOS / WORK

The doctor - El doctor/a/a

The nurse - Enfermero/a

The engineer - Ingeniero/a

The pompier - Bombero/a

The policeman - El/La policía

The dentist - El/La dentista

The manager - El/La gerente

The secretary - Secretario/a

The lawyer - El/La abogado/a

LOS ANIMALES / ANIMALS

The dog - El perro

The cat - El gato

The bird - El pájaro

The bunny - El conejo

The horse - El caballo

The cow - La vaca

The pig - El cerdo

The sheep - La oveja

The mouse - El ratón

LOS ANIMALES SALVAJES

The tiger - El tigre

The lion - El león

The elephant - El elefante

The giraffe - La jirafa

The crocodile - El cocodrilo

The bear - El oso

The dolphin - El delfín

The shark - El tiburón

The whale - La ballena

LA NATURALEZA / NATURE

The tree – El árbol
The flower – La flor
The grass/lawn – El césped
The mountain – La montaña
The forest – El bosque
The sea – El mar
The beach – La playa
The sky – El cielo
The insect – El insecto

The ocean – L'océan

LOS VERBOS / VERBS

To go – Ir (Ir a + verb/location)
To eat – Comer
To sleep – Dormir
To drink – Tomar / Beber
To play – Jugar
To watch/See – Ver
To do – Hacer
To read – Leer
To write – Escribir

ADJETIVOS / ADJECTIVES

Tall/Big – Grande
Small – Pequeño/a
Nice/Kind – Simpático/a
Fast – Rapido
Good – Buen/Bueno/a
Happy – Feliz
Pretty/Handsome – Hermoso/a
Easy – Fácil
Hard/Difficult – Difícil

TRANSPORTE / TRANSPORTATION

The car – El carro / coche
The truck – El camión
The motorcycle – La motocicleta
The train – El tren
The plane – El avion
The bicycle – La bicicleta
The boat – El barco
The bus – Le autobús
The subway – El metro

ACTIVIDADES / ACTIVITIES

To exercise – Hacer ejercicio
To dance – bailar
To play tennis – Jugar tenis
To run – Correr
To buy – Comprar
To travel – Viajar
To speak/talk – Hablar
To ride a bike – Andar en bicicleta
To swim – Nadar

ENFERMEDAD / SICKNESS

I have a .... ache – Me duele…
I have a headache/ stomachache
–Me duele la cabeza/el estómago
Fever – La fiebre
Sick – Enferma/a
A cold – Un resfriado

EXTRA

With me – Conmigo
With You – Contigo
Also/ too: También

Why – Por qué

Answer key

Page 7

A

2 - dos	3 --- tres
7 - siete	9 --- nueve
1 - uno	6 --- seis
8 - ocho	10 --- diez
4 - cuatro	5 ----cinco

B

tres ---- 3	uno -------1
siete --- 7	cuatro ---4
nueve -- 9	ocho -----8
cinco -- 5	dos ------2
diez --- 10	seis ------6

Page 8

B

11 - once	
12 - doce	
13 - trece	
14 - catorce	
15 - quince	
16 - dieciséis	
17 - diecisiete	
18 - dieciocho	
19 - diecinueve	
20 - veinte	

C

16 --dieciséis
17 --diecisiete
20 --veinte
13 ---trece
15 ---quince
11 ---once
14 ---catorce
19 ---diecinueve
18 ---dieciocho
12 ---doce

Page 13

A

43 . cuarenta y tres

55 . cincuenta y cinco

61 . sesenta y uno

74 . setenta y cuatro

37 . treinta y siete

21 . veintiuno

86 . ochenta y seis

32 . treinta y dos

85 . ochenta y cinco

Page 13

B

120 . ciento veinte

300 . trescientos

16 . dieciséis

501 . quinientos uno

190 . ciento noventa

105 . ciento cinco

7 . siete

12 . doce

450 . cuatroscientos cincuenta

Page 14

1- Hoy es miércoles.	4- Hoy es jueves.
2- Hoy es domingo.	5- Hoy es viernes.
3- Hoy es martes.	6- Hoy es sábado.

Page 15

ABRIL - APRIL	JULY - JULIO
MARZO - MARCH	AUGUST - AGOSTO
MAYO - MAY	SEPTEMBER - SEPTIEMBRE
JUNIO - JUNE	OCTOBER - OCTUBRE
ENERO - JANUARY	NOVEMBRE - NOVIEMBRE
FEBRERO - FEBRUARY	DECEMBER - DICIEMBRE

Page 16

lunes 4 de julio de 1999	Monday, February 24	25/01/2016
14 de agosto de 2004	March 20, 1980	13/11/1954
martes 11 de enero	October 5, 2013	07/08/2009
sábado 14 de octubre	Wednesday, May 6, 2021	21/01/2022
25 de diciembre de 2008	Friday, June 11	14/05/2024

Page 18

He - Él
I - Yo
You (inf.) - Tú
She - Ella
You (for.) - Usted

We - Nosotros
You (pl.) - Ustedes
They (f.) - Ellas
They (m.) - Ellos

Page 19

Yo - Tú - Usted - Él -
Ella - Nosotros - Ustedes -
Ellos - Ellos - Ellas

Page 21

1. es - profession
2. eres - origin
3. son - description
4. es – material

5. es - ownership
6. son - origin
7. es - event location
8. es - before noun

9. es - before noun
10. soy - origin
11. es - profession
12. son - material
13. es - description

Page 23

A
1. está - opinion
2. estan - mood
3. está – health
4. estoy - location
5. está - mood

6. está - opinion
7. está - location
8. está -mood
9. estás - condition
10. está - location
11. estamos - location

B
1. SER
2. ESTAR
3. ESTAR
4. SER
5. SER

6. ESTAR
7. SER
8. SER
9. SER
10. ESTAR

Page 24

A

¡Buenas tardes! ¿Cómo está?
(or **estás** if you're on familiar terms)

B

¡Buenos días! ¿Cómo está?
(You can also add **¡Hola!**)

C

¡Hola! ¿Cómo estás?

Page 25

A
1. ¿Cómo estás?
2. ¿Cómo está?
3. ¿Cómo está?
4. ¿Cómo estás?

B
1. Buenos días. ¿Cómo está?
2. Muy bien, gracias. ¿Y usted?
3. ¡Hola! ¿Cómo estás?
4. Bien, gracias. ¿Y tú?
5. ¡Buenas tardes! ¿Cómo están?

Page 27

1. ¿Cuántos años tienes?
2. ¡Hola! ¿Cómo te llamas?
3. Me llamo ...
4. Tengo dieciséis años.
5. ¿Cómo se llama usted?
6. ¿Cuántos años tiene?
7. Tengo veinte años.
8. ¡Adios! ¡Nos vemos!
9. ¡Hasta luego!

Page 28

- ¡Hola! Me llamo Lisa. ¿Cómo te **llamas**?

- **Me** llamo Adam. **¿Cómo** etsás?

- Muy **bien**, gracias. ¿Y **tú**?

- **Estoy** bien, gracias.

. . . .

- ¡**Buenos** días Señora López! Cómo **está** usted hoy?

- **Estoy** muy bien, gracias señor García. ¿Y usted?

- **Muy** bien, **gracias**!

Page 33

For **Connect** and **Translate** see p.32.

La sala	**La** cochera
El inodoro	**La** habitación
El baño	**Las** escaleras
La cocina	**El** jardín
	La casa

Page 36

For **Connect** see p.35.

A

La computadora
La silla
La ventana
La televisión

El sillón
La puerta
El refrigerador
El teléfono
La cama

B

Mi televisión	**Tus** sillas	**Mi** puerta
Tu sillón	**Mi** ventanas	**Tu** teléfono
Mi cama	**Tu** computadora	**Mi** refrigerador

Page 31

For **Connect** and **Translate** see p.30.

La familia	**La** abuela
El tío	**El** abuelo
El hermano	**La** tía
La madre	**La** hermana
El padre	

Page 34

1. Mi familia está en la sala.

2. Mis tías están en la habitación.

3. Mi madre está en la cocina con tus hermanas.

4. (Ellos) Están en la cochera con mi padre y tus hermanos.

5. (Yo) Estoy en mi habitación con mis hermanas y mi abuela.

6. Tu abuelo y mi tío están en tu casa.

7. (Nosotros) Estamos en el jardín con tu familia.

Page 38

For **Connect** see p.35.

A

El lápiz	**La** lapicera
El cuaderno	**La** tarea
El libro	**El** escritorio
El sillón de clase	**El** profesor

B

Tu lápiz	**Tu** escritorio	**La** estudiante
Tu profesora	**Mi** tarea	**Mis** cuadernos
Tus libros	**Mis** lapiceras	**Mi** salón de clase

Page 39

A

Su cama	**Nuestros** cuadernos
Tu teléfono	**Nuestra** profesora
Sus profesores	**Nuestro** sillón
Mi madre	**Nuestras** lapiceras

B

Su padre	**Nuestra** cama	**Sus** hermanas
Nuestra profesora	**Su** habitación	**Su** casa
Sus libros	**Nuestros** hermanos	**Su** madre

Page 40

Mi amiga	Mis amigos	Mi prima
Tus amigos	La gente	La persona
Tres personas	Mis primas	Su amiga
Sus primos	Sus amigos	Nuestros primos

Page 41

1. Mis amigos están en mi habitación.
2. Su hermano está con nuestros primos en la cochera.
3. Mi padre está en la sala con mi madre.
4. Hoy, estoy en la escuela con mis amigos.
5. Sus hermanas están en el jardín con mi abuela.
6. Lisa está en la cocina con sus amigas.
7. Me llamo María y soy estudiante.
8. Los estudiantes están en el salón de clase con su profesora.
9. Su computadora y sus libros están en mi habitación.
10. Mi tío y mi tía están en la casa con mis primos.

Page 46

1. **Le** duele la cabeza.
2. **Me** duele el estómago hoy.
3. Estoy enfermo, tengo un resfriado.
4. Estamos enfermos, tenemos fiebre.
5. **Me** duele**n** los ojos.
6. Mi padre está enfermo, le duele la cabeza.
7. **Te** duele la mano.
8. **Le** duele el estómago, (ud.) está enfermo.
9. (Él) está enfermo. Tiene fiebre y tiene un resfriado.

Page 43

For **Connect**, see p.42.

1 - tiene   6 - tengo
2 - tienen   7 - tienen
3 - tienen   8 - tenemos
4 - tiene   9 - tienen
5 - tienes   10 - tengo

Page 45

For **Connect** see p.44.

A
• **La** mano • **Los** ojos • **El** cuerpo
• **El** estómago • **Las** piernas • **La** cabeza
• **La** nariz • **Los** brasos • **La** boca
• **El** pie

B
Sus pies **Tu** cabeza **Su** braso
Tu nariz **Su** boca **Su** pierna
Mis ojos **Mi** estómago **Nuestras** manos
Mi cuerpo

Page 48

• Rojos • Azul • Anaranjadas
• Verdes • Negra • Amarillo
• Blancas • Rosados • Marrón (or café)

110

Page 49

1. Tengo dos piernas y dos manos.
2. Sus ojos son verdes.
3. (Tú)Tienes una cocina amarilla.
4. Mi casa es marrón y blanca.
5. Su cama es azul pero su habitación es rosada.
6. Tenemos dos libros rojos y tres lapiceras verdes.
7. Mi computadora y mi cuaderno están en tu habitación.
8. Me duelen la boca y la nariz.
9. Mi hermana tiene ojos azules.
10. Tengo un escritorio negro pero mi silla es roja.

Page 51

»» For **Connect** and **Translate** see p.47.

»»
- **La** falda
- **La** camiseta
- **El** abrigo
- **El** pijama
- **Los** pantalones
- **El** vestido
- **La** ropa interior
- **Los** calcetines
- **Los** zapatos

Page 53

»» For **Connect** and **Translate** see p.49.

»»
- **Los** bebés
- **El** desayuno
- **Las** mujeres
- **Los** niños
- **La** cena
- **Las** niñas
- **Los** hombres
- **El** almuerzo
- **Los** niños

 Niño/niña is for younger kids. For a teen/ young adult: muchacho/a - Chico/a

Page 54

1. La niña tiene un vestido amarillo.
2. La mujer tiene un bebé, es un niño.
3. ¡Es hora del desayuno! ¡Ven aquí!
4. Los niños tienen zapatos azules.
5. Sus pantalones son negros pero su abrigo es blanco.
6. Es hora del almuerzo. Vengan aquí, es hora de comer!
7. Su familia tiene una casa marrón (café) y un carro rojo.
8. Es hora de cenar. ¡Ven aquí!
9. Me duele la cabeza hoy.
10. Mi hermano está enfermo, le duele el estómago.

Page 56

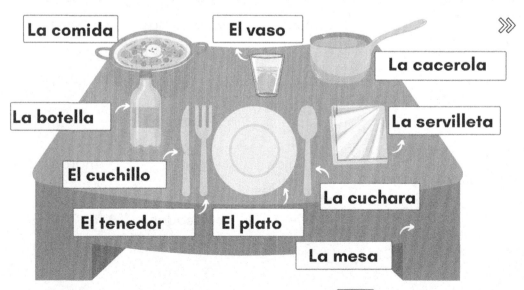

La comida · El vaso · La cacerola · La botella · La servilleta · El cuchillo · La cuchara · El tenedor · El plato · La mesa

»» For **Translate** see p.55.

- **El** tenedor
- **La** comida
- **El** plato
- **La** cacerola
- **La** botella
- **El** vaso
- **La** servilleta
- **El** cuchillo
- **La** cuchara

Page 58

For **Connect** and **Translate** see p.57.

- **El** pan
- **La** carne
- **La** leche
- **El** pescado

- **El** arroz
- **El** pollo
- **La** pasta
- **El** agua
- **El** huevo

Page 59

A

- unas
- una
- un

- unos
- un
- una

- una
- un
- una

B

- una
- una

- unas
- unos

- un
- un

C
1. unos
2. un
3. una
4. unas

Page 60

A
1. Una hermana
2. Una madre
3. Unos estudiantes
4. Una computadora
5. Unas escaleras
6. Una cocina
7. Un brazo
8. Una nariz
9. Un jardín
10. Un baño
11. Una mano
12. Unas casas
13. Una cabeza
14. Una pierna

B
1. un poco de pan
2. un poco de carne
3. un poco de de pollo
4. un poco de arroz
5. un poco de agua
6. un poco de pescado

C
1. **una**
2. **un**
3. **un**
4. **un**
5. **una**
6. **una**
7. **una**
8. **un**
9. **unos**
10. **unos**

Page 61

1. En la cocina, hay un poco de comida en el refrigerador.
2. Hay cinco vasos y unos platos en la mesa.
3. La comida está en la mesa. Vengan, es hora de comer.
4. En mi plato, hay carne y arroz. Quiero comer.
5. Los tenedor**es** y las cucharas están en la mesa.
6. Hay leche en la cacerola.
7. Quiero comer algo ahora.
8. Hay vasos y agua en la mesa.
9. Quiero comer un poco de pescado y un poco de pan ahora.
10. Hay pollo y arroz en el refrigerador.

Page 62

A
1. – ¿Cómo está Miguel?
   – Está bien.

2. – ¿Cómo está la comida?
   – Está deliciosa.

3. – ¿Cómo está el pollo?
   – Está perfecto.

B
- Qué
- Dónde
- Por qué
- Dónde
- Por qué

112

Page 64

》 For **Connect** and **Translate** see p.53

- **Un** melocotón
- **Una** manzana
- **Una** pera
- **Una** naranja
- **Un** plátano
- **Una** sandía
- **Una** fresa
- **Un** limón
- **Unas** uvas

Page 66

》 For **Connect** and **Translate** see p.65

- **Una** cebolla
- **Un** tomate*
- **Una** zanahoria
- **Un** pepino
- **Una** papa
- **Unos** chícharos
- **Una** lechuga
- **Un** maíz
- **Una** calabacita

* Mexico: **Jitomate**

Page 68

》 For **Connect** and **Translate** see p.67.

- **un poco de** té
- **un poco de** queso
- **un poco de** ensalada
- **un poco de** leche con chocolate
- **un poco de** helado
- **un poco de** papas fritas
- **un poco de** jugo de naranja
- un poco de pastel
- **unas** galletas

Page 69

1. Quiero un poco de helado con fresas y un plátano por favor.
2. Quieren agua y un poco de comida ahora.
3. ¿Quieres algo? – Sí, quiero una manzana verde por favor.
4. Para el almuerzo, quieren pan con queso y una ensalada.
5. ¿Quieres un poco de jugo de naranja para el desayuno? – No, gracias.
6. Ahora queremos unas galletas y leche con chocolate, por favor.
7. Para la cena, quiero un poco de carne y chícharos por favor.
8. Quiero un poco de pollo y arroz por favor.
9. ¿(Ud.) quiere un poco de té? – Sí, por favor. Gracias.
10. ¿(Él) quiere pescado y verdura para la cena?

Page 73

》 For **Connect** and **Translate** see p.72

- **El** hotel
- **El** edificio
- **El** cine
- **El** restaurante
- **El** museo
- **La** tienda
- **La** calle
- **El** hospital
- **El** supermercado

Page 75

For **Connect** see p.72

- **La** dentista
- **El** secretario
- **El** policía
- **La** enfermera
- **El** gerente
- **La** doctora
- **La** ingeniera
- **El** bombero
- **La** abogada

Page 76

1. Hace buen tiempo hoy. ¿Te gusta la primavera?
2. Me encanta el verano porque hace calor y me gusta el sol.
3. Hace buen tiempo en primavera pero a veces hay un poco de lluvia.
4. Hace calor en verano pero me gusta el verano.
5. Me gusta el invierno porque me encanta la nieve.
6. Tengo frío hoy pero me encanta la nieve. ¿Le gusta el invierno?
7. No me gusta el verano porque hace calor. Me encanta el otoño.
8. No me gusta el otoño y no me gusta el invierno.
9. En otoño, hace un poco frío pero me gusta la lluvia.
10. Hace buen tiempo hoy. Tengo calor pero me encanta el verano!

because: - porque

why: - por qué

Page 77

Remember to use **ser** when describing someone's profession.

1. ¿Vas a casa? -Voy al parque. No voy a casa.
2. Tu padre es gerente y tu madre es dentista.
3. Mi tía es enfermera y mi tío es ingeniero.
4. La mujer es abogada y el hombre es bombero.
5. Mi hermana es secretaria y mi hermano es policía.
6. No voy a ser profesor, voy a ser abogado.
7. Hay doctores y enfermeros en el hospital.
8. Su padre y sus niños están el el parque hoy.
9. Estoy en la escuela hoy pero mi hermana está a casa. Está enferma.
10. Quiero ser enfermera o doctora.

Page 79

>>> For **Connect** and **Translate** see p.78

- **Un** perro
- **Un** gato
- **Un** pájaro
- **Un** conejo
- **Un** caballo
- **Una** vaca
- **Un** cerdo
- **Una** oveja
- **Un** ratón

Page 81

>>> For **Connect** and **Translate** see p.80

- **Un** tigre
- **Un** león
- **Un** elefante
- **Una** jirafa
- **Un** cocodrilo
- **Un** oso
- **Un** delfín
- **Un** tuburón
- **Una** balena

Page 83

>> For **Connect** and **Translate** see p.82

- **Un** arból
- **Una** flor
- **Un** césped
- **Una** mantaña
- **Un** bosque
- **Un** mar
- **Una** playa
- **Un** cielo
- **Un** insecto

Page 85

>> For **Connect** see p.80.

- **Un** carro
- **Un** camión
- **Un** avión
- **Un** tren
- **Una** motocicleta
- **Una** bicicleta
- **Un** barco
- **Un** autobús
- **Un** metro

- Un autobús amarillo
- Un barco grande
- La motocicleta negra
- El metro
- El carro rojo
- El avión grande
- La bicicleta verde
- El tren
- Un camión negro

Page 86

1. ¡Tienes muchos animales en tu casa!
2. ¿Te gustan los animales? Sí, me gustan mucho los animales.
3. Hay un carro blanco en la cochera.
4. Me encantan los animales pero no me gustan los tiburones.*
5. En el mar, hay tiburones, ballenas, delfines* y peces.
6. En mi ciudad, hay edificios, un hospital y un supermercado.
7. En mi calle, hay muchos restaurantes y un cine.
8. Me gustan los caballos y los vacas pero no me gustan los cerdos.
9. Hay muchos pájaros en el cielo hoy.
10. En mi calle, hay muchos carros, motocicletas y camiones.

(!) *Loses it's accent in the plural.*
(Also: car = coche/ garage = garaje)

Page 88

>> For **Connect** and **Translate** see p.87.

- Quiero leer
- Quiero dormir
- Quiero ver
- Me gustaría hacer...
- Me gustaría ir...
- Me gustaría escibir...
- ¿Quieres jugar?
- ¿Quieres tomar algo?
- ¿Quiere comer?

Page 90

>> For **Connect** and **Translate** see p.89.

- Voy a jugar tenis
- Voy a hacer ejercicio
- Quiero correr
- Me gustaría comprar una casa.
- Me gustaría andar en bicicleta.
- Me gustaría viajar.
- ¿Quieres hablar?
- ¿Quieres nadar?
- ¿Quieres bailar?

Page 92

For **Connect** p.91

- Un primo simpático
- Una mujer hermosa
- Una casa grande
- Niñas pequeñas
- Una buena profesora

- Un carro rápido
- Un niño feliz
- Un examen difícil
- Un examen fácil

Translate:

- Es muy rápido
- Es muy difícil
- Simpática
- Grande
- Feliz

- Es muy pequeño
- Es muy bueno
- No es muy fácil
- Un hombre hermoso

Page 93

1. Mi hermano también quiere ir al cine contigo.
2. ¿Quieres comer un poco de helado ahora? - ¡Yo también!
3. Quiero ir a casa. Quiero leer mi libro en mi habitación.
4. (Él) Quiere hacer su tarea en su escritorio.
5. Me encanta bailar. ¿Quieres bailar conmigo ahora?
6. !Estoy muy feliz! ¡Hoy mi tarea es muy fácil!
7. Ven aqui por favor. Quiero hablar contigo ahora.
8. ¿Te gusta tomar leche para el desayuno? (or "beber")
9. ¡Su carro es pequeño pero muy rápido!
10. Me encanta hacer ejercicio y nadar. A veces, también me gusta correr.

Page 94 - FINAL QUIZ

1. En el bosque, hay osos, pájaros y conejos.
2. Tenemos un perro negro y un gato blanco en nuestra casa.
3. En mi habitación, hay una cama grande, un escritorio negro y una computadora.
4. Soy un buen estudiante. Tengo mis libros, mi lapicera y un cuaderno.
5. En su casa, hay un jardín grande y una cochera.
6. (Ellos) Tienen una televisión grande en la sala.
7. ¡Hola! ¿Cómo estás? Me llamo Sam, ¿y tú?
8. Hoy es miércoles. ¡Tengo un examen difícil en la escuela!
9. Estoy enfermo hoy. No tengo fiebre pero me duele el estómago.
10. Mi edificio es muy grande pero mi casa es muy pequeña.
11. Quiero ir a mi habitación ahora. Quiero dormir en mi cama.

12. Mi padre es muy grande, es bombero.

13. Mi tío es dentista y mi tía es profesora.

14. Mi hermana tiene diez años. Es hermosa y muy simpática.

15. Hay pollo, arroz y chícharos en su plato. ¿Quieres comer también?

16. Quiero una manzana y quiero tomar (beber) un poco de leche por favor.

17. ¡Hay un insecto pequeño en la cocina!

18. Me gustaría viajar con unos amigos en verano.

19. Me encanta tomar leche con chocolate en invierno. (or "beber")

20. Sus niños son muy hermosos. ¿Cómo se llaman?

21. ¡El pollo está muy bueno! Me gustaría comer un poco mas por favor.

22. Para el desayuno, quiero un poco de jugo de naranja y pan con huevos.

23. Para la cena, quiero pasta, un poco de queso y una ensalada por favor.

24. Para el almuerzo, hay papas, calabacita y carne.

25. Su carro es muy grande pero no es muy rápido.

26. Tu abuelo y tu abuela están en su casa.

27. ¿Por qué hay muchos pájaros en el cielo hoy?

28. En verano, estoy muy feliz porque hace buen tiempo.

29. No me gusta el tiempo hoy porque hay mucha nieve.

30. ¡Es muy fácil! ¡Vengan conmigo!

31. Hay mucha gente en el metro hoy. No me gusta.

32. ¿Dónde están mis calcetines negros y mis zapatos rojos?

33. ¡Me encanta la naturaleza pero no me gustan los insectos!

34. ¡Mi tarea es muy difícil! ¡Y tengo mucha tarea hoy!

35. ¿Quieren ir al cine conmigo hoy?

36. ¿Por qué quieres ir al supermercado? – Porque quiero comprar galletas.

37. A veces me gusta ver la televisión en mi habitación con mi hermana.

38. Mi primo tiene un carro verde y una motocicleta amarilla.

39. Quiero comprar calcetines, pantalones y ropa interior en la tienda.

40. Me gustan los trenes y los aviones porque me encanta viajar.

41. En invierno, me gusta jugar en la nieve con mi familia.

42. ¿Vas al parque? ¿Quieres jugar fútbol conmigo?

43. Me gustaría comprar muchos libros porque me encanta leer.

44. Hoy quiero hacer un pastel para mi madre.

45. Voy a la playa con mi familia y unos amigos.

46. Me encantan las montañas y el mar. La naturaleza es hermosa.

47. Me gusta mi escuela pero no me gusta hacer mi tarea.

48. ¡Tengo calor hoy! No me gusta el tiempo en verano. Me gusta la primavera.

49. A veces voy al parque porque me gusta jugar y andar en bicicleta.

50. ¡Me encanta hablar español!

 because now, you can actually speak some Spanish!

THE END!

¡EXCELENTE!

Made in the USA
Coppell, TX
17 July 2025

51997399R00070